D1006178

DISCARD

Renew

Your Marriage

at Midlife

# Renew

# Your Marriage

# at Midlife

•

*Steve Brody, Ph.D., and*

*Cathy Brody, M.S.*

G. P. PUTNAM'S SONS

NEW YORK

**HOUSTON PUBLIC LIBRARY**

R0l134 44l03

Except for the personal experiences of the authors, all cases and characters
in this book are composites from acquaintances and clinical work. Names and
details have been changed to protect privacy and confidentiality.
This book is not intended as a substitute for advice from a trained counselor,
therapist, or other mental health professional. If you are currently in counseling
or therapy, check with your mental health provider before altering or
discontinuing your therapeutic regimen.

G. P. Putnam's Sons
*Publishers Since 1838*
a member of
Penguin Putnam Inc.
375 Hudson Street
New York, NY 10014

Copyright © 1999 by Steve Brody and Cathy Brody
All rights reserved. This book, or parts thereof, may not
be reproduced in any form without permission.
Published simultaneously in Canada

Library of Congress Cataloging-in-Publication Data
Brody, Steve.
Renew your marriage at midlife / by Steve Brody and Cathy Brody.
p.    cm.
Includes index.
ISBN 0-399-14457-9 (alk. paper)
1. Marriage.   2. Middle age.   3. Middle-aged persons—Sexual behavior.
I. Brody, Cathy.   II. Title.
HQ734.B8393      1999              98-36483 CIP
306.81—dc21

Printed in the United States of America

1   3   5   7   9   10   8   6   4   2

This book is printed on acid-free paper. ♾

*Book design by Chris Welch*

# Acknowledgments

We stand on the shoulders of many, some of whom we consider giants. The late Carl Rogers was certainly one. He taught us how to listen and be courageous enough to be ourselves. Tom Gordon showed us how to teach communication skills. Bob Alberti and Michael Emmons defined assertiveness.

When we put together our first marital communications program in 1975, Alan Solomon and Roger Sherwood were instrumental in its creation.

We wish to thank the following colleagues for their help with this manuscript: Writer Beverly Engel recommended us to our incredible superagent, Jillian Manus, and her personable and professional associate, Jandy Nelson. Our ebullient editor, Jeremy Katz, at Putnam and his cheerful assistant, Elizabeth Himelfarb, have been responsive, diligent, encouraging, and supportive.

Thanks, also, to our many clients and workshop participants whose courage and wisdom were the inspiration behind this book.

Finally, we thank our friends and neighbors in Cambria, California. How lucky we've been to raise our children and journey through our middle years surrounded by a sense of belonging and community as natural as the ocean, pines, rolling hills, and creeks of our fair town.

# Contents

We dedicate this book to our parents,
Walter and Roslyn Brody and the late Jack and Mildred Stanley,
and to our children, Justy and Matt.
Thank you for teaching us trust, perseverance, laughter,
and, most of all, love.

# PART ONE

# The Challenge of Change

*

To every thing there is a season,
and a time to every purpose
under heaven.

—Ecclesiastes

### CHAPTER 1

# The Four Seasons of Marital Change

Mid-way along life's journey,
I found myself in a dark wood.
—Dante

Karen was ready to walk out. After twenty-three years of marriage and two kids, she felt angry, lost, and alone. "Now that the kids are gone, the silence between Ron and me is unbearable!" she complained. She tried begging and nagging over the years. She even left him alone for a few months, but nothing had worked. Now as she sat with him in our office, she said counseling would be her last effort.

As she worked her way through a box of tissues, Ron fidgeted with a pillow on the couch, looking shocked. "I knew she wasn't happy," he ventured, "but how could she think of ending the marriage?" It seemed that Ron was a good provider, a good dad, and had remained faithful despite frequent trips away from home as a computer programmer for a large corporation. He couldn't understand what more Karen could possibly want from him.

"He just doesn't get it," Karen continued resentfully. "He'd rather work, stare at the damn TV, or play golf with his brother—anything but be with me." Then she broke down and sobbed. "It's been like this for years. Just me and the kids. And now that they're leaving home, I'm even more lost and alone. I'm forty-five years old. With our youngest about to graduate high school, I've decided to get on with my life, with or without Ron."

Ron looked hurt as Karen grew quiet. Then in a detached voice she described a scenario we hear over and over again in therapy. "I went back to work and began to find myself, but I drifted further from Ron. Now I'm totally lost. I think Ron would be content to continue along the way we are, but I'm not. I'm unhappy. I know I need to do something. But I don't know which way to turn."

Sound familiar? Don't be surprised if it does. Marriage at midlife often passes through such transitions. In Ron and Karen's case, their transition had reached crisis proportion. It's at just such junctures that couples lose their way along the marital journey.

Even if your particular path through the forest isn't as dark as Ron and Karen's, if you've entered midlife or beyond, you know how easy it is to get lost in the woods. You may have felt your relationship lose its way a time or two over the years.

The good news is that with increased awareness and communication, you and your partner can blaze a new path of renewed direction and intimacy as you continue your journey through your middle years.

❋

**It's normal to get lost midway along the marital journey.
Successful couples are those who can renegotiate a new
direction when they hit such critical relationship junctures.**

❋

## Forging a New Marital Path at Midlife

This book is about why we lose our way as couples and how we can forge a new path with our partner through that sometimes dark wood of midlife relationship change. Before we can clear a path out of the woods, however, we first need to get our bearings. Part 1 helps light your way through the forest so you can assess the lay of the land and evaluate which path might be right for you and your relationship. Like standing on a hilltop, it will give you some distance and perspective on your journey.

It's normal to lose your way now and again, especially when you hit big areas of dramatic change. Often at these key junctures along the path of a shared life, the relationship map you and your spouse share becomes outdated. You reach the end of the blazed trail and have to find your way through uncharted wilderness. Like Ron and Karen, you feel stuck and lost until you find a new map to guide you through the next section of your journey.

You face a second complication as well. Your new map may have several routes on it. You and your partner must agree on the path to follow. Can you walk it together? What if you take different paths but plan to meet up ahead? And what if one of you gets lost: Do you have a plan to reconnect?

All this requires negotiation, especially if one or both of you have a change of heart as to your destination—a likely occurrence considering you've traveled the same path together for several years.

Later along the marital journey the early paths you traveled no longer run paralell; they branch off and create problems. Perhaps you're bored and need a change. Maybe your partner has taken ill and can't keep up the pace. Or, like Karen, you might feel lost and lonely when the kids begin to leave home.

On the positive side, if you've pulled a wagon with children who now have left the nest, new paths you couldn't fit down now begin to look inviting. Your marriage is a long journey, and you're likely to hit several of these relationship junctures along the way.

*We certainly have in our twenty-eight years together. As we often say to couples we work with, we're in our fourth marriage to our first partner. Our first eight years without kids were fundamentally changed after two children arrived in two years.*

*Soon after we drew our second map to get us through diapers, little sleep, and even less sex, our marriage changed for the third time and began to revolve around soccer games, mortgages, and balancing the demands of my full-time practice with a full-time family and Cathy's return to graduate school.*

*We're now negotiating our fourth map as our kids, like Ron and Karen's, leave the nest. Suddenly it's just us again. Who are we now as individuals and as a couple? Do we still have common interests and goals now that our lives are not wrapped around our children? We've been looking to the needs of our family for so long that we wonder just who our fellow traveler has become.*

There are two ways to go about relationship change at midlife: either change how you talk to yourself, or change how you talk to your partner. Talk to yourself differently about what you expect from your relationship, for instance, and you significantly increase your marital satisfaction. Your expectations may be based on an outdated map.

But change isn't only an inside job. Sometimes you need to change your relationship by talking more effectively with your partner, especially during key times of marital transition. For example, perhaps you pulled the relationship along while your partner rode and now you no longer wish to pull more than your share. Or years ago you were willing to ride while your partner held the reins, but now you wish to steer yourself.

Changing the rules of the game can trigger resentment, and you or your partner can react angrily. "I thought we had a deal," you might grumble. "How could you do this to me!" you might complain as your partner rips up the old marital map.

❋

**It's normal to feel angry or resentful when your partner
changes during the middle of your marital journey.
The key to negotiating these transitions
successfully is communication.**

❋

*Such resentment and anger surfaced in our marriage when our youngest son entered kindergarten and Cathy enrolled part-time in a graduate program to earn a license as a marriage and family therapist. After seven years of being a mother and a home-*

*maker, she was hungry for more adult stimulation and eager to return to professional life.*

*I had grown accustomed to her being the support person at home. But now she needed me to take care of the kids in the evening while she went to class. I felt abandoned and put-out, while Cathy resented that I felt that way to begin with, expecting me to be more understanding.*

*It's not that I was wrong for feeling the way I did. It's just that change takes time to adjust to, and I had grown used to a certain division of labor. First, I had to become more aware of my feelings of abandonment and anger, not only in the present, but how those emotions stirred up similar feelings from childhood, when both my parents worked full-time while I was still relatively young.*

*After I became clearer within myself, I had to communicate effectively with Cathy as we wrangled over our relationship map at this juncture. Two keys here (and we'll get into this further in part 3) were how Cathy and I dealt with anger and how we as a couple negotiated our conflict of needs.*

*It's important to remember that when your partner changes, it's usually not done to hurt you, although that may be one of the results. As we often say to couples, intention and impact are two vastly different sides of the same coin. One spouse's intention becomes another's impact. Cathy didn't intend to abandon me, but nonetheless the impact of her actions hurt.*

*For my part, I didn't intend for her to feel unsupported, but that's the impact my behavior had on her. It's not uncommon during midlife to feel cheated or betrayed by your mate's change of direction.*

A frequently quoted passage in the Bible reads, "To every thing there is a season, and a time to every purpose under heaven." This is certainly true in relationships as well. Just like the change of seasons, your relationship will inevitably evolve over time, and you or your partner will likely change direction or purpose in life.

❋

**Change is inevitable; it's how you handle it that counts. Don't take your spouse's change as a personal affront or rejection. It often has more to do with your partner and less with you.**

❋

## The Four Seasons of Marriage at Midlife

There are four key "seasons" to most marital midlife transitions. Understanding these pivotal times can help you cope more effectively with your marital disappointment and frustration when your relationship changes.

### *Season #1: Kids Off to School, Mom Out the Door*

One of the most common and challenging midlife junctures is when the last of your children heads off to begin school. Since some people marry or have children later in life, this can hit couples in their mid to late thirties. As you saw with us, Mom often reevaluates her identity or direction in life. It's a time of great opportunity for most women, but it can be a dangerous time of transition for their marriage as well.

This is especially true if a wife harbors resentment toward

her husband for not being more available when the kids were little. Frequently, women enter counseling because of this resentment, sometimes bringing their husbands along for the ride. Our experience working with couples shows that when someone decides to end a relationship at this point, it's more likely a wife than a husband.

If either of you feels lost at this juncture, the good news is that there are two specific things you can do to create a new map for your relationship. First, make your marriage more of a priority.

## PRIORITIZE YOUR RELATIONSHIP

Take time out from being Mom and Dad to go out every Saturday night as a couple, or get the kids to bed at a decent hour so you can have some quiet time together during the evening. This can be especially important for your sex life, which may have taken quite a hit when the kids were little.

Prioritizing the relationship is particularly crucial for men. It's the single most effective thing husbands can do to prevent a midlife marital crisis. Men, you will be amazed by what you see if you just take a look around. It will not come naturally, however, especially during the kids' middle years. That's when many men are busy building careers, making their mark in the world, and providing for the family.

A husband's path can diverge dramatically from his wife's during this time. Husbands often are so busy hacking their way through the forest that they forget to turn around to see if their wives are still on the same trail with them. When men finally do, they're often surprised to find that the women have found their own path.

❋

**Don't lose your marriage at midlife amid the demands of family and career. Make your relationship a priority; it's especially important for men to do so early on.**

❋

It's sad but extremely common to see husbands finally come in for counseling, only to hear from their wives that it's too little too late. The trick for men is to prioritize the relationship on an emotional and conversational level, for it's not enough to be only a provider. Sure, many men wake up to this fact somewhere in the middle of the marital journey, but those who do so sooner rather than later have an easier time of it.

Here's a suggestion: Check in as soon as you notice any distance, and listen to the signals your wife is sending. The odds are that by the time you've noticed them, your wife has been feeling that way for quite some time.

## TAKE GOOD CARE OF YOURSELF

The second way you can salvage your relationship at this key transition point is to take better care of yourself as an individual. Many women join exercise classes, for example, which help work off stress, increase self-esteem, and reduce feelings of isolation. Others walk regularly with friends to meet some of their needs for companionship that their work-minded husbands aren't able to fulfill.

Some couples join a church or temple at this stage, which also helps many feel less alone, both spiritually and socially. If you're happy as an individual, you're less likely to resent your partner for following his or her chosen path or feel frustrated by your relationship.

Keep your relationship expectations realistic. For instance, during the early stages of a relationship, men are frequently quite attentive. Don't expect it to continue. While it would be nice if a husband understood his wife's need for conversation and connection, women need to be realistic and remember that the sexes expect different things from a relationship. Men sometimes need to temper their agenda as well to recognize this same fact.

As a husband beats his way through different brush during this stage, you're both likely to spend a good deal of time walking separate paths. Take care of yourself as you walk yours; it will ensure you'll meet up again later.

❋

**Women often set themselves up with unrealistic expectations. To avoid resentment and disappointment at midlife, fulfill some of your emotional needs outside of marriage.**

❋

## SEX: A KEY FACTOR FOR HUSBANDS

Although women are usually the ones who are tempted to rip up the map through the marital woods during this season of relationship change, sometimes it's their husbands. This was the case with Keith and Charlotte. As is typical with men, sex was a key factor.

"I work like a dog, get chewed out for it, and don't even get laid," Keith complained succinctly. He and Charlotte had been married for fifteen years and had two children, the youngest of whom had recently entered first grade. Charlotte had begun substitute teaching, while Keith was in his thirteenth year as a policeman.

"I buy her sexy nighties, and she gets in bed with her flannel pajamas. It's a damn turnoff," he fumed. "And I think it's intentional." Charlotte admitted that she doesn't feel as frequently turned on as her husband, but she also felt it was partly Keith's fault.

"He can't expect me to just turn it on like he does. I'm not built that way," she replied. "Besides, I don't see what the big deal is." Although an honest difference in perception, this can be a serious mistake for a midlife relationship as far as many males are concerned.

The research is clear: As much as we love our kids, children are hazardous to marital health. Studies show that couples with no children score higher in marital satisfaction than couples with one child, and couples with one are more satisfied than couples with two. Like it or not, children drain time and energy from romance and communication.

After years of sexual frustration or feeling displaced by their children, many men grow tired of being on the back burner physically. They also often reevaluate the marriage, now that Mom is able to return to work and take care of herself independently.

It's a dangerous time for men and their relationships, and affairs are common. They're usually not the cause of separation or divorce, but they're often the catalyst. After years of feeling undesired, the new woman is too refreshing an oasis to give up for the parched sands of a dried-up sexual relationship.

Women would be well advised to not underestimate the

importance of sex for most men. Save time and energy for romance, and get the kids to bed early. If you let your husband know you'd like to make love that night, he'll be more likely to help with baths and homework. Surprise him during the day on weekends, and be adventurous; most men love different sexual settings and positions.

To underscore the importance sex plays in an ongoing intimate relationship, especially for men, one study found that the frequency of sexual intercourse was one of only two key factors determining marital satisfaction. The other, incidentally, was the number of conflicts couples had during the course of a week.

❋

**Nurturing a man sexually satisfies his underlying needs for intimacy and closeness in a language he can understand.**

❋

### *Season #2: When You Change, the Marriage Changes*

Whether you begin a new career or beat an old problem like alcohol, when one of you changes, the relationship changes. It's like a mobile hanging from your ceiling; take off or move one part, and the whole mobile becomes lopsided or distorted. Relationships that fail during midlife are often those that don't adapt to a changing marital partner.

Terrence and Carlotta are a case in point. After years of putting up with her husband's drinking, Carlotta decided she'd had enough. She waited until after Christmas, and on January first she acted on her new year's resolution.

She gave Terrence an ultimatum: sober up or ship out. As

is typical with alcoholics, he denied the problem until the end, when she literally packed up his bags and put them on the front porch. Terrence had to spend the next two weeks on a friend's couch.

Carlotta's resolve hadn't jelled overnight. As in many midlife marriages, she became gradually more independent after returning to full-time work six years earlier. She was a take-charge, highly organized woman who was rapidly promoted up the ranks of her computer software company.

Now in her mid-forties, she felt a sense of urgency about her life, a key factor often pushing individuals toward relationship change in their middle years. "If I don't make a move now, one way or the other, it'll be too late," she told us during her first session.

Terrence had come in the previous week. He began therapy almost too late, often the case for alcoholics. When we first saw him, he told us that he hadn't eaten in three days and would lie awake all night obsessing about his misfortune. His goal was clear, however: "I don't want to lose my marriage."

Carlotta held firm, despite her guilt about upsetting their twelve-year-old son, Jason, who blamed Mom for the separation and alternated among being angry at her, feeling guilty about his anger, and being depressed by the absence of his father.

But Carlotta was no longer willing to follow Terrence's drunken path through the marital map at midlife. She had stalked off the page determined to find a new path with or without him. Such individual change triggers relationship change.

In this case, it was a substance abuse problem, but it could be a career change, an affair, a death or illness in the family, or any number of dramatic individual changes that throw the mobile out of kilter.

*

**Relationships are like a mobile suspended from the ceiling. Move one part, and the whole thing changes. Marriages that fail at midlife are often those that don't adapt to change.**

*

## EXPECT CHANGE, AND COMMUNICATE EARLY

Like it or not, if you're the partner of a spouse going through a dramatic change, your life will be significantly affected as well. So how do you handle it when it happens to you?

The first thing to remember is to not fight against growth or deny change. Better yet, expect changes to occur at midlife and work with them. Even though Carlotta had been unhappy with Terrence's drunken behavior for years, she needed to face the fact that her husband was an alcoholic.

"I can't continue to live with his blackouts and slurred speech. It's dangerous and embarrassing. And I can't continue to live with broken commitments," she said one evening when he didn't show up for therapy. "I'm scared, but I need to push ahead with this." She was right, for although change for Carlotta was scary and difficult, she was finally willing to face up to it and meet it head on.

Keep your partner abreast of how you're changing rather than blindsiding him or her later. This was especially important for another couple, Tony and Susanne.

Tony had seen a lot of growth in himself individually over the course of his fifteen-year marriage. He learned to be more assertive at work and had gained considerable self-confidence by stating his ideas at meetings and with supervisors.

As is common, however, this new and improved Tony had not yet debuted within the marriage, and Susanne did not know of her old husband's new side. For her part, Susanne wasn't very good at reading the fine print or picking up subtle messages when he did say something.

✻

**Better to keep your partner abreast of your changing needs and directions rather than overwhelming him or her late in the game. If you're the other partner, be sensitive to cues along the way.**

✻

Tony exploded during our first couple's session. "I've had it. I can't live with your criticism anymore!" Susanne knew he was unhappy, but she was totally caught off guard by how strongly her husband felt about this.

Many men learn to swallow their emotional needs, and Tony was no exception. He wasn't good at letting Susanne know how he felt or what he needed. This key problem was the primary reason why this midlife transition had reached crisis proportions.

It turned out that Tony had been criticized severely during childhood and had married a woman who was also critical. Unfortunately, we tend to reenact old patterns from our family of origin.

Somewhere along our midlife journey we grow tired of putting up with what feels like the same old injustices and disappointments, and we stride off in a new direction, often without informing our partner.

❋

**We re-create dysfunctional relationships because our
sense of familiarity often lulls us into feeling comfortable.
We may also falsely believe that we'll finally get
what we didn't as children.**

❋

Therapy helped Tony understand and voice his needs more clearly and directly. It also helped Susanne listen more effectively. This was no easy task given her marital models, for her mother had been extremely critical of her father. But Susanne was somewhat aware of her own tendency to be critical; she even chose not to have children because she feared how she would be as a parent. After several weeks of intensive training, Susanne learned to listen more patiently, interrupt less frequently, and reduce her bouts of criticism.

## BE FIRM BUT PATIENT: CHANGE TAKES TIME, ESPECIALLY FOR THE PERSON ON THE OTHER END

To successfully negotiate this second season of marital midlife transition, you also must be realistic, patient, and supportive with your partner after you push for change. Remember, you've just thrown some cold water on the old coals. Although from your perspective you needed to do it, expect some noise and smoke. Even if you communicate your needs effectively, your partner will still struggle against the new arrangement for a while.

This was the case with Marilyn and Jacob. Like Tony,

Marilyn had put up with a critical partner. Only in Marilyn's case, her spouse was a tyrant. When her sister's family visited for dinner, Jacob flicked the light switch on and off when he wanted them to go home. In addition, he completely monopolized the conversation and interrupted her at will.

Marilyn put up with it because she believed she deserved no better due to patterns from her family of origin. Her message from her mother was, "You're a bad girl and don't deserve much in life." Her younger brother was the star of the family, while she was pegged as insignificant, partly because she was female. During her twenties and early thirties, she followed the party line, but somewhere in her late thirties, she began to challenge those old voices.

She went to college and became a registered nurse. Soon after becoming head nurse at a major metropolitan emergency room, she began to challenge the old marriage contract she had with her husband. She had already declared her independence financially, but now when Jacob tried to interrupt her during conversations with family and friends, she would politely but firmly assert her right to continue, a pattern we saw emerge early in therapy. "I'm not done yet," she'd say when Jacob would start to interrupt her.

Although everyone encouraged her to divorce Jacob, Marilyn chose to work on the relationship. She was also realistic about how long it would take her marriage to change. After three years of steadily asserting herself, Jacob eventually got the message.

Marilyn was patient and supportive with Jacob during those years as well, but this is not to be confused with being passive and compliant. Marilyn knew that in order to change her relationship, she would have to be firm and consistent.

But she wasn't rude, and she rarely raised her voice. She didn't need to. She was firm in her conviction, and that translated into strength in her negotiations with Jacob. She maintained her personal power without lording it over him.

Marilyn stayed in her marriage but insisted that it reflect the change she had gone through during her middle years. Within the safe boundaries of marital commitment, we all need room to grow and change as individuals. Marilyn had the courage and perseverance to make that change.

❋

**Don't be pushy or aggressive about your changing needs at midlife. Do be firm, consistent, and patient, however. It will take time for your partner to adjust to the new you.**

❋

### Season #3: The Empty Nest: Just Us Again

Another dangerous season of midlife transition is when the kids become teenagers and leave home. Without the children underfoot, many couples reevaluate one another as marriage partners after years of focusing elsewhere.

You or your partner may have changed significantly as individuals during the past ten to twenty years. Perhaps your expectation for how much time you spend together as a couple differs from your partner's. Where do we go from here? you wonder. Well, the answer to that question is often crisis and conflict.

❋

**If your kids are teenagers or have recently left home,**
**you and your partner may be looking at each other across**
**an empty nest wondering, "Now what?"**

❋

## FACING THE EMPTY NEST REQUIRES REALISM, CREATIVITY, AND COURAGE

Now that the girls were leaving for college, Vivian hoped that she and Cal would travel more together. They had married fifteen years earlier, soon after Vivian's twin daughters by a previous marriage turned three.

But Vivian knew it was a long shot, for Cal was a workaholic. He was a successful rancher who loved nothing better than planting a new crop or constructing an innovative drip system. Besides, he hated to travel. This left Vivian, at fifty years old, in conflict.

"I don't feel right just taking off by myself," she confessed. "It seems selfish, what with Cal working so hard out there. But damn it," she said angrily, "at last this is our chance, with Marleena and Melissa now off to school."

Since Cal wouldn't come to counseling, Vivian decided, "It's up to me." A woman friend invited Vivian to join her on an inexpensive walking tour of Montana, and she decided to give it a try. Cal was too wrapped up in his work to care much anyway.

Vivian loved it. When she came in for her next appointment, she was a changed woman in many ways. "I'm my own person now," she beamed, "and I'm excited about the future."

Although she missed Cal during the week she had been away, it was okay once they both got used to it.

"I could make a big scene out of this separate travel stuff," she added, "but why? Why not let Cal be Cal and me be me?" She was right. Vivian and Cal are a good example of realism, creativity, and courage during the middle years, when it's important not to badger your partner to choose the same path as you. Although Cal never came in for therapy, Vivian claimed that he was relatively fine with the arrangement, as long as she didn't spend too much money on travel.

We would do well to follow Vivian's example and allow more space in our intimate relationships. For thousands of years, marriage wasn't a romantic union. It was functional; its purpose was to raise children. Men would leave their wives to dance around the fire with the other men of the tribe, while women would mash corn or sew quilts together. They didn't expect too much from a marriage partner, and they were probably ahead of the game for it.

Vivian walked through Burma and bicycled through Southern France. Cal continued to plant crops and construct new projects on the ranch. Their relationship grew stronger because of the space they had given each other. They now walk different paths for part of the journey and hook up periodically for the rest.

This is not as easy as it sounds. They have to withstand the tongue wagging of others in their small town. It takes courage to walk a path that is uniquely yours.

As the poet e. e. cummings once said during a speech he delivered at Harvard: "To be nobody but yourself—in a world that is doing its best night and day to make you everybody else—means to fight the hardest battle any human being ever fights, and never stop fighting."

*

**Be realistic. Your goals and desires might differ from your spouse's once the nest starts to empty. Have the courage to develop a creative enough solution to meet your and your partner's needs.**

*

## WHEN DISTANCE ERUPTS INTO CRISIS

Leonard and Takako, on the other hand, argued constantly when their kids started to leave home. With their son in college and their daughter a junior in high school, they were right in the middle of their third season of marital midlife transition.

Like many couples, they had lost much of their intimacy early in the marital journey, especially after their daughter was born. Leonard felt cut off sexually and isolated outside the family loop. He threw himself into his work, opening up one restaurant and then another. He was rarely home when the kids were in their middle years. Nonetheless, Takako held the family together and managed their finances frugally.

It was Leonard who cracked first. "I don't know what's happening to me. I think I'm having a nervous breakdown." He wasn't, but he was seriously depressed and highly agitated. He was a classic example of a midlife crisis.

As is often the case, it was his marriage that had triggered the crisis. "I've been walking on eggs trying to please my wife, but I can't go on anymore." He feared getting stuck in a dysfunctional marriage like his parents. "With the kids almost gone," he added, "there's no reason to stay."

Leonard had a point, for that's a key challenge for a marriage at this stage of midlife. Couples correctly realize that with the children gone, one of the big reasons for continuing their union is no longer there. They're free to choose a new path at this juncture along the journey. Many opt for jumping off the map, as Leonard did by filing for divorce.

He regretted it five months later, but by then, it was almost too late. Takako went through hell after receiving the divorce papers, but eventually stabilized. To her credit, she was willing to consider creating a new map with Leonard, albeit cautiously.

The key for this couple was learning to communicate, one of the "Three C's" of a successful relationship. The first C is the initial chemistry of attraction, which includes what the British philosopher Bertrand Russell considered crucial, a similarity of values. The next step along the marital journey is the second C, commitment, which keeps a couple together.

But it's the third C, communication, that keeps you growing as vibrant, intimate companions. This is where Leonard and Takako had failed, especially during the middle years of their marriage. Without communication, they had stayed together in body, but not in spirit.

❋

Of the Three C's of a successful relationship—chemistry,
commitment, and communication—once the nest empties,
it's your ability to communicate that becomes most essential.

❋

Leonard and Takako rebuilt their relationship on the ashes of the old one. The process nearly killed them, literally, when Takako attempted suicide soon after Leonard moved out. With intensive counseling, great determination, and communication training, they eventually got through it, but there are ways you can prevent this third season of marital transition from becoming such a crisis.

## CHANGE IS NATURAL AND HEALTHY

As in the two earlier seasons, recognize and accept the fact that you're at a natural point of transition, rather than pretend that things are still the same and that everything's okay. If you feel confused and anxious at times, don't be too hard on yourselves, individually or as a couple. This is entirely normal when you pass through a key season of transition.

If you have teenagers or adult children who have recently left the nest, don't be surprised if you and your spouse start looking at yourselves or your relationship differently. It's healthy to reevaluate your options and to work toward making some changes, including financial ones.

This doesn't have to be traumatic. Indeed, for many relationships it can be a subtle process involving gradual career changes, more financial planning toward retirement, and exploring new ways of spending time together as a couple.

❋

**It's normal, even healthy, to shed leaves and grow new ones as you pass through this key season of midlife transition. Careers and financial goals may also change as kids empty the nest.**

❋

*When our older son entered college and our younger one started to drive, we suddenly had huge blocks of time we couldn't imagine possible only a year earlier. Instead of taxiing kids to Little League or to the beach, we often had entire weekends for long walks together, sometimes even hiking to town and back for a leisurely lunch or dinner. It was like beginning an entirely new marriage, but with an old friend.*

## COPING WITH
## DIFFERENT COMMUNICATION STYLES

Talk with your partner to clarify and redefine your new roles within the changing family landscape. How successful you are will depend not only on your ability to communicate, but how similar you are in your desires to do so. Studies show that couples with partners who communicate to a similar degree are happier than couples where one spouse wants to share far more than the other.

It's neither unusual nor dysfunctional, however, to have different styles of communicating. Some people are more sensitive to emotional stimulation, while others tend to block it out. For instance, when researchers flashed gory accident scenes on a screen for a fraction of a second, some subjects opened their eyes wider to take in the information, while others narrowed their pupils to block it out. Neither group was more dysfunctional than the other, just different.

If you're the one who likes to communicate and your partner prefers to block things out, don't overwhelm him or her. Pick times when you're both not too tired and knock on the door, so to speak, before entering by asking your partner if this is a good time to talk. Keep it simple, stay focused on one issue at a time, and be brief.

Check your audience periodically during your discussion. If you tend to be a talker and your partner isn't, stop every minute or two to give him or her a chance to speak. You don't want to burn out your listener. Remember, it's to your advantage that your spouse stay in the ring. You're the one who wants to talk, not your partner; so help your spouse by keeping your communications short and to the point.

❋

**If you're the talker in your relationship, don't overwhelm your partner. Keep your communication brief, simple, and focused.**

❋

If you prefer less communication than your partner, be gentle with him or her. Remember how important it is for your companion to share thoughts and feelings and to learn what you think about the relationship, especially now that things are in flux. If you feel overwhelmed during one of these discussions, say so early on and ask for what you need.

For instance, if you need your partner to slow down, to stick to one issue at a time, or to speak in smaller segments, ask him or her *before* you get angry. An intimate companion is more likely to feel attacked if you wait until you're frustrated, for your tone of voice will likely give your anger away. Then, of course, the damage is done, for as the old Chinese proverb says, "Not the fastest horse can catch a word spoken in anger."

If you need to take a break during a conversation to prevent exploding, do so, but give your partner a definite time when you'll return to the subject at hand, like over dinner or after you go for a walk.

❋

**If you talk less than your partner, remember that his or her needs are different. When you take a time-out during a discussion, give your spouse a specific time you'll reconvene.**

❋

Finally, explore potential activities and hobbies you might enjoy together as a couple. Don't go to the mat arguing over things that your partner obviously doesn't enjoy. Brainstorm until you come up with one or two activities that are mutually enjoyable. If you like tennis and your partner doesn't, and he or she likes golf but you can't stand it, don't do a hard sell on either one. Keep them as special individual activities.

Instead, push ahead on sure winners. For instance, if you both like to walk or go out to dinner and a movie, do those more frequently. Generate a list of new possibilities as well, including things you both enjoyed earlier in your relationship.

If the two of you skied, played backgammon, or cooked together when you were younger, why not try them again? You'd be surprised at how much fun you can have as a couple now that the kids are gone, provided you do things you both enjoy.

### Season #4: The Marital Challenges of Aging

Finally, we have the fourth season of marital change, which comes at the end of midlife: the process of growing older. Aging can stress your relationship because it often brings difficult transitions with it, like sudden health problems or on-going disabilities.

You and your partner will likely lose family members and close friends, or you may feel less powerful, productive, or independent. These in turn can lead to depression.

## RETIREMENT CAN DEPRESS HUSBANDS AND CHALLENGE MARRIAGES

Soon after Raymond turned sixty, his wife Terecita brought him in for counseling when he talked about driving his truck off a cliff. Mourning the loss of his youth, Raymond felt useless since his retirement five years earlier as a successful executive in the insurance industry.

"I'm like an old bull elephant without any tusks. They might as well shoot me," he said sadly. "I'm even a burden to my wife," he added, which was somewhat true. His depression kept him at home, and Terecita was afraid to leave him alone.

Raymond was a classic case of an aging male on the downside of his middle years. His loss of productivity wounded him to the core. If he was not the successful provider, who was he? Was he worth anything? He didn't think so, and he felt as if he was being dragged kicking and screaming from midlife into old age.

❋

**Men often feel less worthy, powerful, and productive after retiring as providers. Their loss of identity and prestige can trigger depression as well as marital stress and conflict.**

❋

Raymond's depression was a case in point; it definitely challenged his wife Terecita. She had faithfully followed his lead during their marital journey by raising their three children and taking care of the home. But she was also used to a lot of independence.

Having Raymond underfoot was stretching her ability to be tolerant, and she was beginning to resent his depression and lack of activity. She also felt stifled by his constant presence. Raymond sensed it and felt unwanted. Marriage during this season of transition can be especially challenging because it often throws an older couple together for more hours than they can handle, especially when one spouse is having difficulty adjusting to retirement.

❋

**By the time a wife grows comfortable with the marital distance often set by her husband, he retires and gets underfoot at home, leaving her to lament, "For better or worse, but not for lunch!"**

❋

This was true for Raymond and Terecita. They finally were able to work it out, after Raymond recovered from his depression, that is. The key was helping Raymond come to terms with his sadness over the loss of his early adulthood. By talking it out, he saw how unrealistic it was to hold onto the past and how he needed to face the sobering realities and challenges of this new transition in his life: growing older.

He was then free to enjoy his retirement, which he began to do with gusto, becoming heavily involved in community activities. As is true for many couples, once the troubled partner successfully completes the transition, the relationship often returns to a previously comfortable and well-worn path.

## HEALTH ISSUES ALSO
## CHALLENGE OLDER COUPLES

When her health started to fail at fifty-eight, Erma grew increasingly dependent on her husband, Leroy. This was in sharp contrast to their early middle years, when both of them worked full-time and had a successful marriage.

Now, however, they were like two animals in a small cage. They began to turn on each other as conflict gradually replaced the affection that once flourished between them. Leroy was beside himself. "I don't know what to do. I can't leave her, but she's driving me crazy."

The solution was to return to something that had worked earlier: They needed more space and independence. Leroy overcame his financial frugality and sprung for a part-time caretaker for Erma. As had been the case with Raymond and Terecita, once the mobile was back in balance, the transition from the middle years to beyond was complete.

❋

**Health issues become more frequent as couples reach the end of midlife. Such problems throw the marital mobile off balance, as previously independent spouses grow increasingly dependent.**

❋

## HOW TO AGE SUCCESSFULLY AS A COUPLE

We should point out, however, that most couples make the transition from their middle to later years quite well, thank you.

According to a study in the journal *Psychology and Aging*, the resolution of important conflicts in older marriages "was less negatively emotional and more affectionate than in middle-aged marriages."[1] The older couples had learned to control their tempers more effectively, and they were less likely to escalate a conflict once they had one.

So take a lesson from the research. Hold back on the negative emotions and handle your conflict with more patience and affection. The researchers also concluded that one reason older couples argue less is because they have learned to leave well enough alone over the years. Not bad advice for the rest of us. Remember that making it through the transition is the hard part.

❋

**According to the research, older couples are less angry, disgusted, belligerent, or whiny with each other compared to couples in their middle years.**

❋

Other studies show four key traits that separate successful older couples from those who don't negotiate this final midlife transition well. First, and not surprisingly, you need to maintain a strong sense of commitment. Don't threaten separation or divorce, for once that is broached, anxiety floods in, and repairing trust becomes a slow and difficult task.

Second, share your feelings with your partner. This is crucial if you want to maintain intimacy. Successful older couples grow closer over the years, and this is especially important when it comes to sex. Erection difficulties and health problems won't necessarily end your sexual relationship if you can communicate effectively with your partner.

Third, develop your friendship with each other. Studies show that while some of the early heat of romantic passion may lessen over the years, many older couples excel at being good "companions at love." Once again, you can deepen your intimate relationship despite the often difficult challenges of growing older.

Finally, be flexible. One recent study found that couples who were flexible and able to adapt to stress and change were more likely to be satisfied with their relationship during their later years. They also fought less than those who weren't as flexible.[2]

❋

**Successful older couples affirm their marital commitment, maintain an intimate relationship, develop their friendship, and learn to be flexible with each other.**

❋

To sum it all up, you need to be aware of the changing seasons of marital transition during your middle years. Hurdles that occur during these key periods present normal, but nonetheless difficult challenges.

It's easy to lose your way along the marital journey when you're either broadsided by dramatic events or surprised by the gradual accumulation of change. Either way, at some point things shift just enough and the whole picture changes. If you're prepared for the normalcy of such changes, you'll be better able to handle them.

In the next chapter we'll show you how to read the warning signs of marital midlife crisis and what you can do to cope with them. Then in part 2 we'll help you avoid the key marital myths you're likely to run up against during your middle years. We'll also share with you how you can talk to yourself more realistically and positively about your relationship.

In part 3 you'll learn how to effectively negotiate the relationship differences that inevitably emerge during midlife, how to prevent conflicts from erupting, and how to de-escalate them when they occur.

Finally, in part 4 we'll talk more specifically about changes in your sexual relationship, including menopause, erection difficulties, and affairs. We'll also offer some tips to help handle being sandwiched between exiting children and aging parents and help you cope with the challenges of work and retirement.

### CHAPTER 2

# The Warning Signs
# of Midlife Crisis

Peace is easily maintained;
Trouble is easily overcome before it starts. . . .
Deal with it before it happens.
Set things in order before there is confusion.

—Lao-tzu

Marguerite called for a therapy appointment because she had trouble sleeping and felt anxious and depressed but didn't know why. Her marriage began to look like the culprit, however, after she said, "Now that the kids are gone . . ." twice during the first three minutes of the session.

"One moment I get along with my husband, and the next moment I can't stand him," she added, beginning to describe a functional but distant second marriage of fourteen years. "Since our youngest went away to school last September, I've been jumpy and on edge."

At forty-seven years old, Marguerite was also beginning to experience the early stages of menopause, which contributed to her sleep problem and her feelings of jumpiness and volatility. Her doctor had given her hormones, which helped to a certain degree, but Marguerite was also experiencing an identity crisis. She needed to sort out who she was and where she wanted to go now that her role as mom had ended.

Marguerite's case raises three fundamental questions concerning relationships at midlife. First, if you're having a marital midlife crisis, how do you identify the symptoms or warning signs?

Second, how can you tell when your dissatisfaction is due to your own individual transformation at midlife or when it's due to the stagnation of your intimate relationship?

Finally, when should you work on your relationship and when should you throw in the towel? This is one of the toughest and most common decisions facing many couples during a marital midlife crisis. In this chapter we'll answer those three questions and offer some tips to prevent midlife relationship meltdowns from occurring or help you cope with them once they do.

❋

**Three concerns you need to address regarding midlife crises: What are the warning signs? Is it you or your marriage that's causing the crisis? If it is your relationship, can it be saved?**

❋

## Beware of Distance, Depression, and Resentment: The Warning Signs of Midlife Malaise

You say you don't feel much passion or look forward to being with your partner lately? That it feels like one of you has changed or drifted away? Well, the good news is that a certain amount of emotional distance is par for the course for relationships at midlife. The bad news is that it could get out of hand and lead to divorce, depression, or both.

Marguerite was lucky to catch her distance early enough to be able to reverse some of the damage that had already been done to her marriage. She was also fortunate to have a husband who was willing to work with her.

Thomas was visibly anxious when he learned that his marriage was in trouble. His parents had divorced when he was seven, and after already going through a painful divorce during his early thirties, it frightened him to think of losing Marguerite. At fifty-one, he was looking forward to traveling with her in their RV after he retired in a few years.

Marguerite had the three telltale signs of midlife marital malaise: resentment, depression, and distance. Unchecked, they can lead to divorce. Resentment usually appears first. For Marguerite, the resentment resulted from many years of disappointment that Thomas had not been more involved with her and her two children from her first marriage. Tax season was especially painful, when Thomas, an accountant, would work twelve to fourteen hours a day for months at a time.

❧

**Of the three telltale signs of midlife marital malaise—resentment, depression, and distance—resentment usually appears first, often after years of marital disappointment.**

❧

Marguerite was a passionate woman who expressed her emotions openly and without hesitation. This was her strength, but as we often say to clients, a strength overplayed can become a weakness. Thomas's strength was his calm and meticulous persona. In fact, it was these very qualities that first brought the couple together.

When overplayed, however, their styles also frustrated one another. Marguerite was seen by Thomas as overwhelming and hysterical; the more she emoted, the more he withdrew. Thomas's quiet logic frustrated Marguerite, especially when he detached to analyze a potentially emotional issue.

One of the most difficult determinations to make in a marriage is when to voice frustration and disappointment to your partner (and then handle his or her reaction) versus when to work out the problem internally by changing how you look at it or think about it. The key is how successful you are when you choose to work on it privately.

If you're genuinely able to move beyond your disappointment and frustration by altering how you think about the problem, like changing your expectations, for example, then you're unlikely to be left with a reservoir of resentment. But beware of swallowing too many unresolved feelings, for those are the ones that can accumulate and harden into generalized resentment.

In Marguerite's case, the resentment had progressed to the point of triggering the other two warning signs of marital midlife crisis: depression and distance. She felt worthless and despondent a good deal of the time, cried frequently, and had trouble both getting to and staying asleep. Her depression stemmed directly from several years of marital frustration and disappointment, Marguerite felt, for everything else in her life seemed fine.

The final warning sign of Marguerite's midlife relationship crisis was the distance she felt from her husband. "I've built a wall between me and Thomas," she noted. "The good news is I don't get hurt, but I hardly feel anything toward him anymore," she worried. "I don't mind becoming more independent, but I don't want to become so self-sufficient that I don't care about him."

## Coping with the Warning Signs

The first way to cope with these warning signs is to get a handle on your growing relationship distance before it gets the better of you. The marriages we save in therapy are usually the ones that come in early enough.

It's also important to talk to your partner early on, before you become bitter and attacking. The longer you wait, the more likely your communication will be tainted with repressed accumulated anger. When you communicate your needs before you become angry, your tone of voice will be easier to listen to, and you're more likely to be positive.

❋

**Blocked feelings create distance, both within yourself and in your relationship. The earlier you talk them out, especially before they harden into anger, the easier they will be to resolve.**

❋

It also helps to be aware of key gender differences when it comes to relationship expectations. Generally speaking, women romanticize relationships more than men do and are therefore frequently disappointed by their distant mates.

One key to Marguerite's success in turning her relationship

around was changing her expectations of Thomas. She correctly reinterpreted his interests in golf and work as passions that had significant meaning for him, rather than misinterpret and personalize them as proof of how unimportant or unworthy she was as a human being. She also learned to be shorter, more simple, and direct in her communication.

Thomas, for his part, learned to prioritize the relationship. Although that did not come naturally given his gender conditioning, his marriage was important to him, and he was willing to change how he thought about his relationship and how he behaved toward Marguerite. Thomas needed to put more time and attention into both sharing his feelings and listening to those of his partner. By reevaluating their expectations of one another and changing key behaviors, Thomas and Marguerite diffused the resentment that had been building.

❋

**To prevent resentment, depression, and distance, a woman shouldn't misinterpret her husband's lack of connection as lack of caring, while men need to be more attentive emotionally.**

❋

### *Are You Friends with Your Spouse?*

Finally, to prevent or cope effectively with these midlife relationship warning signs, keep building your intimacy as a couple. Although previous studies showed that intimacy, passion, and commitment are the three key ingredients to a successful marriage, a recent study compared those three and found that intimacy is more important than the other two.[1]

When the researchers interviewed over one hundred couples about what kept them together and what led to their marital satisfaction, intimacy, such as liking each other and sharing feelings, was the best predictor of marital satisfaction for both husbands and wives. Passion was second. And although commitment didn't result in marital satisfaction, it did keep couples together and was especially important for husbands. Passion, incidentally, decreased over time for wives. The researchers concluded that "if you truly consider your spouse a friend, you are far more likely to enjoy a long, happy marriage with that person."

*

**Although previous studies showed that intimacy, passion, and commitment are the three key ingredients to a successful marriage, a recent study found that intimacy is most important.**

*

If friendship is such an important ingredient for a long and happy marriage, as the researchers in the above study concluded, we need to explore what it means to be a friend. For openers, at its root the word friend means "to love." Assuming you're lucky enough to have your partner as a friend, do you also love your spouse?

The dictionary goes on to say that a friend is "a person attached to another by feelings of affection or personal regard." Do you show your partner that affection? When your spouse is upset, do you give him or her a hug? Do you pull up a chair to listen, as you might for a friend? In short, do you treat your partner as you would a good friend? If not, make more of an effort to do so, for it's crucial if you want to rekindle your relationship at midlife.

Besides having feelings of affection for your partner, the definition of a friend also includes "a person who gives assistance, a supporter." Do you do that? If a friend called and needed a hand, you'd probably go out of your way to help rather than say "no." Do you extend the same effort toward your partner when he or she needs your assistance or support?

Finally, consider the dictionary's third definition of a friend: "One who is on good terms with another; one not hostile." Do you let your resentments accumulate, or do you work to get beyond your hostility toward your partner? Do you say you're sorry or admit that your partner may be right now and then?

✻

**Research shows that if you consider your spouse a friend, you're more likely to have a long and happy marriage.**

✻

If you need to raise the level of intimacy in your relationship, remember that friendship requires effort, so spend fifteen minutes of uninterrupted time each day sharing personal thoughts and feelings. It's also important to listen to each other. Whether you talk about your job or the kids, it's your commitment to sitting down together as a couple that counts.

Another way to enhance your friendship is to develop activities of mutual interest. Have fun together! Branch out and try something new or perhaps something you did as a couple years earlier. This is especially important for marriages during their middle years, when relationships frequently feel stale or stagnant. For some couples, trying something new might mean a dance or cooking class, while for others, enjoying a good movie together might be the ticket. Be flexible, keep trying, and be creative.

❋

**Rekindle your relationship by spending time together and exploring new activities as a couple. The bottom line: Put some fun back into your marriage, especially at midlife.**

❋

Enrich your life as an individual as well. Let's not get carried away and imply that everything has to be done as a couple. If you grow as an individual, you become less dependent on your spouse for fulfillment, and you mature into a more interesting partner along the way.

## COPING WITH DEPRESSION

So far we've talked about recognizing the warning signs of a marital midlife crisis and ways you can enhance your relationship, but what if you're already moderately or severely depressed? Well, the first thing to do is to talk to a therapist or your physician to get a handle on just how serious your depression is.

If you *are* depressed, get back to basics: that means eating right and getting enough sleep. Sleep deprivation alone, by the way, can cause emotional and relationship problems. Research and clinical experience show that exercise is one of the best things you can do to pull yourself out of a funk. It's free, you can schedule it just about anytime, and it doesn't have any negative side effects.

Social support is also important, so make an effort to get

together with friends and family. Studies show that they literally can be good medicine. As psychologist Joan Borysenko, the author of *Fire in the Soul*, told us recently: "When we feel good about ourselves and connected with others, when we can give and receive love, both the immune system and the cardiovascular system work their best."

Choose your support people wisely, however; the last thing you need is to be around toxic people. Also, don't burn out your friends. If you're depressed, you're not going to be much fun until you get better, so scatter your shots to prevent exhausting one or two friends or family members.

Consider medication as well if you're moderately to severely depressed. Studies show that antidepressants alone often are as helpful as counseling. If there is a biochemical component to your depression, which we believe often occurs after prolonged periods of stress, like a dysfunctional midlife relationship, for example, antidepressants can be especially helpful.

●

**If prolonged marital stress has caused you to become depressed, double up on your exercise and social support, and explore medication and counseling.**

●

Studies also show that two particular forms of counseling are especially helpful in the fight against depression. One is called cognitive therapy, which teaches you how to talk more effectively with yourself. The bottom line here is that how you think creates how you feel.

If you "catastrophize" or "awfulize" about your life by saying things to yourself like, "My life is horrible and will never get any better," you'll likely follow those thoughts with feelings of despair, helplessness, and hopelessness. The good news, as we'll talk more about in part 2 of this book, is that you can learn to change how you think about your relationship at midlife, and as you do, change how you feel.

The other form of counseling teaches you how to take effective action to clear relationship hurdles. This includes many of the communication and assertion skills we'll focus on in part 3. As the writer Ralph Waldo Emerson used to say: "Lose yourself in action lest you wither in despair."

Your relationship with God or the larger scheme of things can change how you feel as well, even if your midlife marital malaise hasn't crescendoed into a depression. An increasing number of studies show that spirituality can be powerful therapy.

In one study, those who attended church regularly were four times less likely to commit suicide than those who didn't attend at all.

In another study of almost a thousand hospital patients, only 17 percent of those who were involved with their religion a great deal suffered from depression. Of those who weren't involved very much, 35 percent were depressed—that's twice as many.

❋

**Spirituality can be powerful therapy. Even if you're not clinically depressed about your marriage at midlife, prayer and meditation can help you cope with disillusionment and loneliness.**

❋

So, how can you use spirituality to protect yourself against or help you deal with depression? First, consider prayer or meditation. Second, if you're not traditionally religious, take quiet walks in the hills or by the sea. Finally, get together with others who believe as you do.

"Patients and their physicians who get in touch with their spiritual resources do better," said Dr. Nancy Dickey, president of the American Medical Association. "They have less pain after surgery. They get better quicker. They find diseases cured. In medical terms, their morbidity and mortality improve."

Clinical depression aside, however, developing your spiritual resources is an excellent way to quiet yourself down and restore your sense of equanimity and well-being, especially when the realities of life during the middle years fail to meet your expectations. This strategy can be particularly helpful when you feel disappointed or frustrated in your intimate relationship.

## Is It Me . . . or My Marriage?

Sometimes it's not your relationship that needs to change, but you as an individual. Oftentimes it's both. That was the case with Neal the year his kids began to leave home, he turned fifty, and he inherited enough money to retire in a few years. Suddenly he wasn't the same person he had been for the past twenty years; he wasn't a dad, a provider, or a young man anymore.

"It was when that damn AARP card came in the mail," he reflected. "That's when it hit me that I'm no longer young. I mean, there it was, in black and white. My youngest kid got her driver's license telling her she was old enough to drive, and I got a card from the American Association of Retired Persons telling me I'm old, period."

Neal ran out and bought the loudest Harley-Davidson motorcycle he could find and screamed down the road toward the open spaces of Montana for a week. Even without the inheritance, he had made almost enough money during his career as a stockbroker to retire, but inside he felt like a failure.

### The Reawakening of Childhood Issues

You might be surprised that Neal had any problems at this point. After all, he had enough money to retire, he was in good health, and his kids were starting to leave the nest, freeing him to travel for the first time in twenty-five years.

But dramatic individual change, even if positive, can trigger an identity crisis. Underneath this cataclysmic social redefinition of who Neal was as a man, a subtle but psychologically more profound drama was unfolding. Old images of when he was a child now began to haunt him.

❀

**Is it you, or is it your marriage that needs changing?**
**Frequently it's both, as old issues, often from childhood,**
**reach critical mass, propelling us forward in new directions.**

❀

All Neal's life he had struggled with the need to be important, to be seen and recognized. When he was four years old, his mother gave birth to a sister, who died only six months later. His mother went into a deep depression and withdrew from the family. Young Neal lost not only a sister but, more important, a mother who had previously adored him.

He referred to this lost little boy as "Needy Neal," who became desperate for affection and substituted what he couldn't get at home with the attention and recognition he soon found at school. He acted out for that attention during grammar school by misbehaving, but later received his fix of recognition by bringing home A's on his report card for his mother. She appreciated his academic success, for no one in the family had finished high school, let alone gone on to college.

Neal, however, graduated with honors from UCLA, joined a successful brokerage firm, and served as president of several volunteer organizations. But with each accomplishment, the quick fix of recognition didn't last, for no matter how hard he tried, he couldn't fill the void that was at the heart of Needy Neal.

On his motorcycle trip to Montana, he met a woman and had a torrid affair. He began to question his marriage, and his unhappiness and loss of meaning and purpose in life left him clinically depressed. His wife, Jan, had been patient, but after six months of living with Neal's depression and irritability, she too was growing restless. A couple who should have been thrilled to begin a new marital journey had reached the end of the road.

Neal resented Jan because he didn't feel she had been affectionate enough during their marriage. What became clear
to him, however, was how he unfairly blamed her for his feelings of being unloved. Once he recognized that much of the
responsibility for feeling unloved was his—because of his
early childhood issues—he reevaluated his plans to separate
from her.

Jan, for her part, was surprised at how sad and lonely Neal
had felt in their relationship and realized that her focus on the
kids and the family's finances had left her with little time or
energy for their marriage over the years.

❋

**We all react to one-alarm blazes as if they're four-alarm**
**fires on occasion. Feeling unloved, for instance, may have**
**less to do with a partner's behavior, and more to do**
**with our own unmet needs.**

❋

### Midlife Can Trigger Spiritual Quest

The combination of individual and marital therapy helped,
as Neal gradually began to pull himself out of his midlife
crisis. For him it was also a spiritual transformation — spiritual in the largest sense of that term, for although Neal didn't
participate in any organized religion, he did feel a sense of rev-
erence for what he jokingly referred to as the Force from the
*Star Wars* movies. He felt especially connected to Mother
Nature.

It's often this burgeoning of spirituality that provides the key to successful transition and renewal during the later middle years. The renowned psychiatrist Carl Jung once said he had not met one patient whose cure, in the final analysis, did not come down to some larger, spiritual understanding.

For Neal it meant letting go of pumping up Needy Neal with trophies and accomplishments and embracing a subtly but profoundly different way of approaching the world. Rather than tighten his muscles, hunch his shoulders, and do battle with the world, he began to listen to his body, take life one moment at a time, and approach each day with the faith that it would work out.

"Faith, not fear" became Neal's motto as he opened to the world rather than squinting fearfully at it. When he let go of struggling to wrest enough attention and recognition to quiet Needy Neal, his neck and shoulders began to relax, and his marriage loosened and became more intimate.

Because he was less needy within, he was less dissatisfied with his marriage. He began to see Jan for who she was, rather than as only a vehicle to meet his needs for love and recognition. In short, he was completing his personal midlife transformation, and as he did so, his marriage was able to continue its journey as well.

❋

**The less needy you are within,**
**the less dissatisfied you'll be with your marriage.**

❋

Thinking of your marriage as sacred, by the way, also can strengthen your relationship, according to a recent study.[2]

Couples in what researchers defined as "sanctified" marriages reported more marital satisfaction, greater commitment, and better ways of handling conflict compared to couples who did not think of their marriages as sacred.

One possible reason is that spiritually oriented couples believe that there is a higher presence within the marriage. This belief may help them stay committed to each other, as well as the spiritual force that holds them together. In addition, the researchers concluded that "couples who sanctify their marriages may have more religious and spiritual resources to handle the ups and downs of daily married life."

Those couples in sanctified marriages, by the way, were not necessarily traditionally religious, according to the researchers.

## When to Work on a Relationship, and When to End It

Stephanie knew she was unhappy but couldn't put her finger on why. At forty-eight years old, and with her youngest daughter recently out of the house, she had become increasingly frustrated with her husband, Dwayne.

"My marriage was never the greatest, but now everything he does drives me crazy," she lamented. "I haven't been happy for years. What really scares me is that I'm not sure I want to stay married to him. But I can't imagine a divorce. All the things we've been through together. What would I tell the family? The kids? How would I survive financially?"

Then she raised two questions we often hear from frustrated husbands and wives during their middle years: "Should

I stay married?" and "How can I tell when it's over?" Answer the second one, and the first one will follow.

## How Can I Tell When It's Over?

Although there are no easy answers, there are things you can do to help find a sense of direction. Most important, you need to assess how much feeling you still have for your partner.

Stephanie, for example, had no affection left. "You can stretch taffy only so far," she said, "and at some point, it snaps." That was her metaphor for reaching her breaking point. You must take a hard, honest look at yourself on your deepest emotional level, and then have the courage to act in congruence with how you feel.

❋

**Whether or not you end your marriage at midlife will likely depend on how much emotional connection and warmth you feel toward your partner.**

❋

A therapist can help you sort through your feelings, examine how realistic your expectations are, and sift through your options, but when it comes to measuring your emotional connection with your partner, you're the one who knows you best. The same holds true for family and friends, who often can provide excellent feedback, largely because they know you so well. But the buck stops with you—which is one reason why this process of exploration is so painful and why it takes such tremendous courage to act. For, despite your confusion and uncertainty, you're still the best person to determine whether you should stay married. No one else knows the pieces of this shattered marital jigsaw puzzle better than you.

Besides gauging how much feeling you have left, another question you should ask yourself is whether or not you still can make love to your partner. If you can't, or if you recoil from your partner's touch and have felt this way for at least six months, our experience says that it will be difficult for you to rekindle enough emotional warmth to be able to renew your relationship at midlife.

A common exception to this rule, however, is the couple who wrestles with sexual dysfunction as their principal complaint. Here the sexual distance is less a reflection of a relationship on its deathbed and more a problem that can be treated successfully in therapy.

❋

**Your sexual feelings are a good barometer of how you feel about your partner, for although the mind can lie, the body usually doesn't.**

❋

Keep in mind that marriages are not as predictable as mathematics or physics. There are few hard and fast rules, and relationships, like the rest of life, are crap shoots, subject to the laws of probability.

For instance, we've seen marriages renewed that we thought never had a chance. At the same time, however, you don't want to hang on for too long after the party is clearly over. Living in limbo can be painful and detrimental for all concerned.

With that said, though, it's also important for you to be realistic about your relationship expectations at midlife. Don't expect fireworks and lots of passion after twenty years together. For most couples, that probably won't happen.

But don't underestimate the value of a shared history, extended family, and your spouse's strong points, like loyalty, a good work ethic, or whatever else your partner brings to the table. It's your choice to divorce, but you need to be realistic about whether the gain's worth the pain, for pain there will be, should you decide to divorce at midlife.

### Deciding Not to Renew Your Relationship at Midlife

Assuming you've given divorce considerable thought and you're ready to take the plunge, let's walk you through what you might expect and offer you some do's and don't's when it comes to ending a relationship during your middle years.

First, you're unlikely to be 100-percent convinced that divorce is the right option. Usually there's plenty of guilt, anxiety, and ambivalent feelings to go around. Take action anyway. The longer you live in limbo, the more frustrated you and your spouse will become.

Your partner probably will be caught by surprise when you drop the bomb, and although you may have spent the last year or two letting go, your spouse probably has just begun. We've seen many a partner, frequently the husband, caught off guard when hit with the "D" word. Divorce may have been the farthest thing from your partner's mind, so be prepared for an emotional reaction.

❋

**Your partner will likely be six months to two years behind
you emotionally. Although you've been letting go
for quite some time, your spouse has just been
hit with the shock of a divorce.**

❋

He or she will likely react with disbelief at first, and then
make Herculean efforts to woo you back. Don't be surprised
if this angers you. "Now he's trying, when it's too late!" you
might remark either out loud or to yourself.

Be firm and consistent during this period, for your partner
will likely mistake friendship for intimacy and a desire to
renew the marriage. You could say, "How are you," for instance,
and your partner might hear it as "I still care about you." Be
patient; it will take a few weeks or months for your partner to
get the message.

When he or she does, that's when the fireworks typically
begin. Your spouse probably will get angry, and from his or her
point of view, rightfully so. You're abandoning ship, and your
spouse feels unjustly rejected. "How could you do this to me?!"
your mate might throw at you in anger. "What about the children?!" he or she may demand, the tone being one part question and nine parts accusation.

Despite the obviously barbed intent, this question is
nonetheless important. In one study on children of divorce,
about a third of the kids were affected disastrously, another third so-so, and a third were better adjusted than
kids from intact families. When researchers looked at why
the last group developed so well, they found two key factors.
First, the kids weren't drawn into the parental war, for

the divorce process between their parents was held to a dull roar.

Second, the kids that did well after a divorce also did not lose a parent. Custody was shared effectively, and because the parents were able to cope with their anger, the children were not blocked from continuing relationships with both of them.

&#42;

**Research shows two key factors affect children of divorce: (1) how the parents cope with their anger, and (2) whether a child loses a parent because of the divorce.**

&#42;

You're likely to be vulnerable to affairs or new relationships during the time between letting go of the marriage yourself and finally telling your partner about it. This is another reason for taking action sooner rather than later, for your partner's anger is more likely to be volatile if you meet someone new early in the game. It's hard enough on your mate to be dumped; it's salt in the wounds to be replaced. If in your heart you know it's over, take action to end your relationship early. Also, should a new relationship become serious too early in the game, your children are likely to hold your new partner responsible for the breakup of your marriage, which will endanger the stability of your future stepfamily.

One of the challenges and opportunities of midlife is that it can push you off the known map of your relationship. It's easy to lose your way or lose sight of your partner as you forge ahead in such uncharted territory. It's also easy to misinterpret the early warning signs of individual midlife transition as symptoms of marital dissatisfaction.

If you're unsure whether it's your relationship or something else in your life that needs changing, consider changing other things first, like your job, for example. If you're depressed, try counseling or medication.

It's normal at midlife to reevaluate your path, and you will likely rip up an old map or two along the way. But as you revise the road ahead, give your partner a chance to join you on your new journey.

# PART TWO

# Self-Talk

*Change Your
Expectations
at Midlife*

✦

We do not see things as they are.

We see them as we are.

—Talmud

### CHAPTER 3

# How Unrealistic Expectations Ruin a Relationship

Two men look out through the same bars:
One sees the mud, and one the stars.
—Frederick Langbridge

What you think creates how you feel. This was at the root of Eileen's dissatisfaction with her husband, Roy. After eighteen years of marriage, her expectations of him were still unrealistic, so she was forever disappointed.

When she suggested going out to dinner at a particular restaurant, Roy responded, "That place is too expensive, and we don't have a coupon. How about Chinese food?" Eileen was furious. All she could see was how cheap and unromantic he was.

"He never initiates going out," she complained, "and if I make the plans, he wants to use one of those damn two-for-one coupons. I hate those things!" As is common with such marital conflicts, it's not the issue itself, but the meaning we bring to it that's most important. Eileen reacted strongly because she took Roy's suggestion of Chinese food as a personal rejection. "If he really loved me," she reasoned, "he would take me to an expensive restaurant."

As a poet once wrote: "Two men look out through the same bars: One sees the mud, and one the stars." Eileen saw only the mud in her midlife relationship. She rarely saw stars. Roy was hardworking, a good father to their twelve-year-old son, Casey, and although he was frugal, he was willing to go along with his wife's desire to go out to dinner.

Eileen's marital dissatisfaction was due more to her unrealistic expectations and less to her husband's shortcomings. Such faulty thinking, however, is unfortunately not uncommon. It's at the root of much of the marital disillusionment and divorce that destroys many relationships during the middle years.

*

**There are two ways to change your relationship at midlife: either change how you talk to yourself (your marital expectations) or change how you talk to your partner.**

*

## Don't Let Anyone Pull Your Marital Strings

How you talk to yourself is due partly to the messages you receive from the culture at large about what to expect in an ongoing intimate relationship.

Take Snow White, for instance. How many wives at midlife

still unconsciously expect to be awakened by the kiss of a handsome prince (or the star on the twelve-o'clock soap opera, for that matter)? Eileen does, although she's not aware of it. Nonetheless, it's at the root of much of her marital dissatisfaction.

She waits expectantly for her husband Roy to bring her to life, and if he fails to initiate a show of affection, she feels cheated and disillusioned. Of course, she becomes "disillusioned"! Her expectations are based on illusion to begin with, not on the realities of marriage at midlife.

Her husband, Roy, however, has a different screenplay in his head. His cultural heroes are men of action first, and if they win the hand of some fair maiden, it's usually as an afterthought. He remembers playing catch as a kid growing up in New York, where he would fantasize diving to the ground like his idol, Willie Mays of the Giants, saving the game in the bottom of the ninth inning.

Inside the minds of these marital players at midlife are two very different movies. When their partners don't play out the parts they're expected to play, disillusionment leads to dissatisfaction.

❋

**Many unrealistic expectations are cultural myths, like the classic fairy tale where a handsome prince awakens Snow White with a kiss. The problem is, we forget they're only fairy tales.**

❋

Your beliefs and assumptions about your relationship at midlife are also influenced by how you were treated as a child.

Mental health professionals call this transference: the tendency to transfer expectations from the past onto the present. Expect to be abandoned, rejected, criticized, or controlled, and you up the odds you'll see that in your marriage. Psychologically, believing is seeing.

How your parents treated each other will also influence how you behave and what you expect from your partner, for we often model or do the opposite of what our parents did in their relationship. Although Roy hated how his mother always told his father what to do, unconsciously he kowtowed to Eileen like his dad did with his mom, hoping to win her appreciation. He was also quick to become defensive whenever he felt slightly controlled or dominated.

❋

**What we expect from a relationship, especially regarding core issues like rejection, abandonment, criticism, or control, is dramatically influenced by key themes we learned in childhood.**

❋

## Change Your Expectations to Raise Your Marital Satisfaction

The bad news is that you're preprogrammed more than you realize. But as Gestalt psychiatrist Fritz Perls once said, "Awareness, per se—by and of itself—can be curative."[1] The good news is that you can learn to spot these emotional land mines, defuse them, and even correct them.

When you do, you change their meaning, and you become less distressed by marital events. You're also triggered less frequently and for shorter periods of time. Your internal reality can change. It all begins with how you talk to yourself, your thinking, and what you expect from your partner and your marriage. In other words, it's time to listen to and change your self-talk.

The research on marital training programs, like the one we do, is also encouraging. First, studies show that you can indeed change your mistaken beliefs and assumptions. And second, as you do, your marriage becomes more satisfying. Learn how to avoid these unrealistic expectations, and you avoid many of the relationship hassles that come with them.

❋

**Reality is largely an inside job. Change how you perceive your relationship and what you expect from your partner, and you dramatically alter marital satisfaction during your middle years.**

❋

There are two common cultural myths and unrealistic expectations about relationships. Sensitivities from your past also can affect your marriage at midlife. Remember: Change how you think and you change how you feel. You can dramatically improve even the most troubled marriage.

## Two Cultural Myths About Marriage at Midlife

Aristotle once said that he who tells the stories controls the minds of the people. This is certainly true when it comes to your expectations about marriage. From *Leave It to Beaver* in the 1950s to *The Cosby Show* in more recent years, marriage at midlife was portrayed as effortless and conflict free.

Add to television all those fairy tales you were spoon-fed during your formative years, from "Sleeping Beauty" to "Snow White," and it's little wonder that deep in your cultural unconscious you probably have some mistaken beliefs about marriage.

If marriage at midlife magically unfolded for Ozzie and Harriet in the 1950s, at least it existed. Those fairy tales you dozed off to when you were young never got that far. The story ended at courtship or perhaps the birth of the first child. You never heard, as Paul Harvey calls it, "the rest of the story."

### *Cultural Myth #1: They Lived Happily Ever After*

Missing something in your relationship at midlife? This myth could be the culprit. If everybody else lives "happily ever after," you reason, what's wrong with us? Well, possibly nothing. What could be wrong is the mistaken belief that you were ever supposed to live "happily ever after." Don't buy it. It'll set you up for failure, frustration, and disillusionment.

This is especially challenging when you hit your middle

years, when time feels as if it's slipping away. Like the title of a collection of short stories by novelist William Saroyan, *I Used to Believe I Had Forever*, you feel a sense of urgency. Happily ever after isn't happening, and you begin to fear it never will.

## WHAT DO YOU WANT? EVERYTHING. WHEN DO YOU WANT IT? NOW!

Another cultural factor setting us up for disappointment is the belief that we are entitled to instant gratification. For the most part, we have more freedom now than ever before. We can move across the country at the drop of a hat, change careers more easily, even get a "quickie" divorce.

But our expectations have skyrocketed as well. We expect freedom from financial anxiety, freedom from sickness and disease, even freedom from marital conflict and boredom. In short, we expect too much.

Most of our grandparents didn't ask marriage to bring them personal satisfaction or emotional fulfillment. They expected to work hard and save for the future. They didn't expect long-term psychological intimacy either, and they may have been ahead of the game for it.

That's not so today. Buy now, pay later, we believe. If you're not happy in your intimate relationship, split, but we forget that while wood and rock split, people tear.

If our mythology says couples should live happily ever after, and our cultural messages reinforce the expectation that fun and fulfillment should happen today rather than tomorrow, then the realities of an ongoing intimate relationship can become downright discouraging.

❋

**Don't expect to live "happily ever after." The more realistic**
**you are with your expectations about marriage at midlife,**
**the greater your relationship satisfaction.**

❋

Somewhere in early midlife you wake up and smell the coffee. The road to marital bliss is an aging freeway, your spouse isn't fun anymore, and the graying picket fence still needs painting. *Father Knows Best* is now Father isn't sure where the college tuition money will come from or how to approach his exhausted, working wife. For her part, she's tired of putting up with years of minimal communication squeezed in between news reports and football scores.

The problem is one part reality and three parts faulty expectations. For the simple truth of the matter is that couples don't live happily ever after any more than individuals do. Throw two people together in close quarters for years on end and you have a relationship that requires ongoing maintenance and, to use an old-fashioned word, work.

## MARRIAGE TAKES TIME AND EFFORT

Simply put, things don't just happen in a marriage at midlife; we must make them happen. It's a capital myth that family life will unfold for us like it does on television. We know this intellectually, but emotionally we continue to expect perfect bliss.

We come home from the office and unconsciously expect our relationships to be candles on the table and long embraces at the door. Yet the reality is that making a marriage work takes as much effort as building a successful business or raising a competent, happy child. It's literally a labor of love, and it demands a serious prioritizing and commitment of our time.

Four of the most common marital hurdles frequently cited by researchers and clinicians are household chores, money, sex, and kids. In-laws or stepfamily relations are a close fifth. But the hidden sleeper in our opinion is time management: setting aside time for your relationship.

We need to align our marital mythology with that of the American work ethic, which says that if you work hard, you eventually succeed. We expect a work hero to put in long hours before becoming a successful oil mogul or newspaper tycoon. Well, it takes an investment of your time to build a successful marriage at midlife as well. This doesn't mean years of marital drudgery and pain. But it does mean taking the time to focus your attention on your partner and the changing needs of your relationship during your middle years.

Falling in love was a piece of cake. Maintaining your ongoing intimate relationship takes more effort. It's different than infatuation, because you know what you have: the good, the bad, and the ugly.

Although the early stages of your romantic relationship were the epitome of illusion, where you saw mostly what you wanted to see, those courtship days also contained ways of relating to your partner that could help renew your marriage today. Remember how polite and considerate you were when you tried to woo or impress your partner? That's exactly the tone you need to re-employ now as you work to rekindle your relationship at midlife.

## SUCCESSFUL MIDLIFE COUPLES
## ADAPT TO CHANGE

Which leads us to another mistaken assumption of the happily ever after myth: that relationships stay the same over the years. Although sometimes true, often it is not, and it can be a core challenge for a marriage during the middle years to realize that your relationship has changed, and not necessarily in the way you wanted.

A successful midlife marriage requires one of the basic building blocks of good mental health: the ability to adapt to change. Acknowledge the transitions you and your partner have gone through and take a realistic picture of your relationship. If you don't like what you see, you may need to risk exploring additional changes. The upcoming chapters will teach the skills you need to learn to be an adaptive spouse, but here are two fundamental rules.

First, catch yourself when you start to get angry at your partner for changing. Acknowledge how this particular transition makes you feel and recognize what triggers your uneasiness. Note how your own thoughts, not necessarily your partner's behavior, contribute to how you feel.

Then, get below your anger to more vulnerable feelings of loneliness, disappointment, or fears of losing your partner. This can be especially challenging when your spouse becomes more independent or less focused on the relationship. As we'll show you in chapter 6, your partner will be more likely to listen to your underlying feelings if he or she doesn't need to defend against an angry attack.

❋

**Marriage takes work. It takes the ability to adapt to change during the middle years as well. To beat the "happily ever after" myth, invest time and effort in your relationship.**

❋

## Cultural Myth #2: Midlife Is the Same for Men and Women

Although you think you don't buy this second myth, you might be surprised at just how differently you respond to midlife depending upon what sex you are. Freud thought it was due to biology. "Anatomy is destiny," he concluded. Others argue that it's your culture that conditions you to respond differently than your partner.

Imagine the following scene, for instance. A young boy is brought into the emergency room after being struck by a car. The surgeon looks down at the operating table and says, "I can't operate on this boy, he's my son." Yet the surgeon is not the boy's father. Take a moment to see if you can explain how this can be before reading the answer.

It turns out that the surgeon is the boy's mother. If you haven't heard this riddle before, don't be surprised if it threw you. It's a good example of how we're conditioned to think of men and women differently. The culture, and to a certain extent our biology, carve out divergent roles, possibilities, communication styles, and even ways of thinking, depending upon what sex you are.

## EMOTIONAL INTELLIGENCE DEVELOPS
## DIFFERENTLY FOR MALES AND FEMALES

These differences emerge early. Boys seem to be more rough and tumble, for example, while girls appear to be nicer, more polite. In one recent study, when a researcher gave boys and girls a disappointing gift and then watched their reactions, the girls pretended to like the gift better than did the boys. "There's greater pressure on girls to be compliant and act nice," the researcher concluded.[2]

By the time you hit kindergarten, parents and teachers expect girls not only to control their emotions more than boys, but to do so with more sophisticated strategies than males.

It's no wonder men and women handle their emotions differently. We even have different kinds and levels of what's called "emotional intelligence," according to another recent study of over 7,500 men and women throughout the United States and Canada. When it comes to self-regard, for instance—your ability to respect and accept yourself as basically good—males score higher than females. They also cope with stress more effectively. But women handle interpersonal relationships better than men, are more responsible and constructive in a group, and better understand and appreciate the feelings of others.[3]

These findings should come as no surprise when you consider how boys from a very young age are trained to be more goal oriented and to overcome obstacles. Girls, on the other hand, are initially more verbally expressive, and they're encouraged to pay more attention to interpersonal relationships.

❋

**Don't expect your partner to respond to midlife like you do. Males start out more self- and goal-oriented. Females initially focus on relationships and how others feel.**

❋

## MEN AND WOMEN DEVELOP DIFFERENT GOALS AND COMMUNICATION STYLES

And you wonder why you and your partner expect different things from your marriage? Or that you express yourselves differently when you try to meet those expectations? As one middle-aged man put it: "Women talk to connect and gather up ideas. My wife asks the same question twelve times to get twelve different inputs, and I stop listening after the second one." He has a point. Women often talk to connect or explore, while men typically use talk as a tool to complete or fix things.

These differences between men and women reflect a fundamental discrepancy in how we approach the world and what we value as important. Men have been programmed from day one to venture away from hearth and home. Their value was measured by how many buffalo or bear they brought back from the outside world.

While a man's worth was weighed by how many skins he carried home as a provider, a woman's, traditionally, was reflected in how successful she was at loving and nurturing others. To a certain extent, Freud was right: Anatomy was destiny. Childbirth and breast-feeding demanded that a woman cultivate the art of connecting with family. Little wonder that the strengths of her emotional intelligence are still her ability to handle relationships and to be empathic with others, whereas a man's still reflect his ability to cope with stress and to respect himself.

## THOSE GENDER DIFFERENCES DIMINISH

Carl Jung did his colleague Freud one better by extending the notion of the masculine and feminine sides of personality. Jung suggested that males and females have the capacity for both, but that typically men allow themselves to experience only the masculine side, while women usually develop only the feminine. Hence, men can express tenderness and empathy too; women can be assertive and task oriented. This also explains why some men may be more in touch with their feminine side than their wives, and vice versa.

If you're in your middle years, additional forces are at work as well. First, you came of age amidst a revolution in what it means to be male or female in this culture. Women are not only keepers of the hearth and supportive caregivers for the family. They now command tanks, play basketball, and run newsrooms.

What it means to be a man is also broader. Not only are they tough providers who compete as they climb the corporate ladder, but they burp babies and nurture preschoolers, activities considered "unmanly" just a generation ago.

A second force to be reckoned with at midlife is the challenge to contribute and to feel productive, what psychoanalyst Erik Erikson called "generativity." "Mature man needs to be needed," he wrote.[4] But when your kids no longer need you, this can be tough, especially for wives.

It's as if your reason for existence was canceled when the

nest emptied. Even your body seems to dry up during this time, and men now look at your daughter rather than you. Because you still "need to be needed," you can feel empty and without purpose at midlife.

This is true for husbands as well. Besides also feeling un-needed by your children, your generativity may have peaked in the workplace. You gradually become less of a player, as younger men and women start to threaten your position.

You feel less career flexibility and a sense of urgency about "making it." Even your body, like your wife's, begins to betray you. Your once dependable erection is now questionable, and young women look past you like you're not even in the game.

## DIFFERENCES BETWEEN MEN AND WOMEN CAN REVERSE AT MIDLIFE

But then a strange thing happens. Somewhere along your midlife journey, you let go of the masculine struggle to make your mark in the outer world, and you turn toward the feminine—hearth and home. As Lane, a fifty-two-year-old criminal defense lawyer in one of our workshops, admitted: "I had enough notches on my gun, and the thrill of battle didn't do it for me anymore. I'm taking a cooking class and puttering up a storm in our garden," he added, "and I can't believe how much fun I'm having."

His wife Carol, however, had already "been there, done that." Having raised the kids and taken care of the home (as well as taught kindergarten), she shifted from taking care of others to taking care of herself. Just as her husband had moved from the masculine to the feminine, she made a U-turn in the opposite direction. She enjoyed visiting her new grandchild, but she loved not taking care of anybody, choosing to walk on the beach with her friends instead.

❋

**Men and women move in opposite directions at midlife.**
**Men explore their feminine side of feelings and**
**relationships, while women increasingly head off**
**to connect with the outer world.**

❋

This can challenge a relationship at midlife. When Carol moved away from her feminine side and let go of taking care of others, Lane felt abandoned. This is not uncommon, for just when some husbands at midlife turn to hearth and home, their wives oftentimes walk right past them as they eagerly head out the door to explore the larger social world. Carol, for her part, both resented Lane's demands on her time and felt guilty for neglecting him.

It helped when they realized that this quandary was fairly normal for a couple at midlife. It also helped to listen to each other. Once they each felt understood, most of the conflict dropped away, and the remainder was easy enough to problem solve.

## Two Family Myths About Marriage at Midlife

Besides the myths you inherit from the culture, you also acquire mistaken beliefs from your family of origin as well. These too are subtly but profoundly embedded in the wiring of your brain. They are not software programs easily erased, and they influence most relationship issues that appear on your screen at midlife.

Take your family's sense of closeness, for instance. Whether you grew up in a close-knit, emotional family or a distant and detached one leaves an imprint on your psyche about what should be the "right" mix of emotion and distance in your intimate relationship today.

The problem, however, is that your partner has an imprint of what that mix should be as well. Such notions of "right" and "wrong" are often at the heart of marital conflict and can definitely impact your relationship during your middle years.

Another hot button is the fantasy that your partner will fulfill you or make you whole. This is less of an issue during the hectic years of career building and child rearing—there just isn't time. However, it's often triggered at the point of a midlife passage when you leave your well-worn path behind and haven't yet chosen a new direction to replace the old.

For instance, if your kids recently left the nest but you haven't yet filled in the void, you're vulnerable to grabbing whatever emotional lifeboat is closest. Unfortunately, often that's your partner, only he or she may not be ready for nor want the job.

Getting in touch with these powerful but often hidden family assumptions frequently can mean the difference between emotional turmoil and domestic tranquillity. The more facile you become at seeing them, the more likely you will be to prevent marital conflict from rocking your boat during midlife.

As the Jesuit theologian Tony de Mello once wrote: "There is only one cause of unhappiness: the false beliefs you have in your head."[5] Free yourself of them, and you renew your marriage, and yourself, at midlife.

*

**Assumptions about intimacy are imprinted in your brain by how you interpret childhood experiences. Renewing your marriage depends on your ability to see through them accurately.**

*

## Family Myth #1: I'm Right, You're Wrong

Imagine an artist, an environmentalist, and a real estate developer all looking at a beautiful, unspoiled beach along the rugged coast of central California. The artist sees how the setting sun illuminates the sides of the pines and oaks dotting the bluff overlooking the ocean. He notices the new shoots of green grass and the orange wildflowers that now cover much of the neighboring hills since the rains began. In short, his mind is awash in colors, shapes, and shading as he takes in the view.

The environmentalist looks at the same coastline but sees a different picture. She wonders how the deer fared during the dry months before the rains and if the trout have returned in the creek. She fears that a proposed resort will forever scar the land, and although she is typically a gentle and peaceful person, she feels unusually angry at the developer who threatens her cove.

The developer, on the other hand, sees it as his land. "After all," he reasons, "my family bought this property many years ago." He envisions beautiful resort hotels and even a golf course overlooking the beach, and he delights in picturing thousands of tourists enjoying the ocean view. When he looks at the cove, he sees building sites, road easements, and bank notes.

Our point here is that although all three gaze at the same stretch of coastline, they literally see it differently. Which one is "right" depends upon your perspective, which in turn is influenced by your values and your history. Like marital conflict, each would argue the righteousness of his or her perspective and would probably have difficulty hearing, understanding, or valuing the opinions of the other.

## SEE YOUR PARTNER'S POSITION AS DIFFERENT, NOT DYSFUNCTIONAL

Eric and Hillary had something more personal on their minds than the California coastline. Twelve years into his second marriage, Eric had pulled away sexually, and Hillary was resentful, lonely, and scared. The more she tried to talk about it, the more Eric withdrew. Eric wouldn't go to counseling, but Hillary insisted that if he didn't at least join her at one of our weekend workshops, she would move out.

"She's always ragging on me," complained Eric, when we dropped in to see how they were doing with one of our listening exercises. He was having a tough time hearing Hillary's perspective.

We suggested that Hillary listen for a while, and as Eric started to open up, it became clear that much of his withdrawal sexually stemmed from feeling angry and overwhelmed by Hillary's expectations for emotional closeness and verbal intimacy.

As is not uncommon, according to one study, the partner who abstains or withdraws sexually often feels overwhelmed and powerless in the relationship. Eric's weapon was his passive-aggressive withdrawal. It seemed like a normal response to him, for in his family of origin, nobody expressed emotion.

Not only was he shell-shocked by Hillary's verbal and physical demands for intimacy, but he genuinely thought Hillary had psychological problems. Previous to the workshop, he confessed, he thought she needed therapy.

Now he began to realize that his emotionally distant and detached family of origin had imprinted him with one set of marital assumptions, while Hillary's verbally expressive and physically demonstrative family had predisposed her to expect something radically different.

*

**Don't assume you're right and your partner's wrong.
You come from diverse backgrounds. Understand and
respect those differences, rather than fight them.**

*

This is more difficult than it sounds, for the temptation to think of your position as somehow more valid, mature, realistic, or right is difficult to check, especially when it's something you feel strongly about. But it's crucial that you do, for if you think of your perspective as the only version of truth and light, you will come across to your spouse as stubborn, arrogant, unyielding, or inconsiderate. Marital understanding, communication, and conflict resolution then become much less likely.

Keeping an open mind is difficult for good reason. Like the environmentalist and the developer looking at the same coastline, you and your partner view the marital landscape differently. When you grapple with sex, kids, in-laws, or money, for instance, you see and understand the wisdom and rationale behind your own opinion.

Your spouse, however, seems to miss the point—your point—and you're tempted to dismiss his or her arguments as illogical, inconsiderate, unrealistic, or wrong. It's as if you and your partner view your marriage and life around you through different glasses.

## THE LOOKING GLASS OF PERSONAL HISTORY

Much of that glass was shaped and ground by early experience. In his psychological bones, Eric believed that family and marital life should be quiet, reserved, and respectful of individual autonomy and independence. Those were the untaught lessons he learned at the knee of his Scandinavian parents. His mother never pressured his father, and his father dutifully provided for the family and quietly took care of the cars and yard.

What was normal, comfortable, and familiar to Hillary was entirely different. Her Italian family was passionate, expressive, and physical. Whereas Eric's parents never kissed or hugged in front of the children, Hillary's dad would affectionately grab her mom from behind as she did the dishes. Dinner was a clamorous cacophony of loudly expressed argument and opinion.

Hillary's expectations of affection and communication were worlds apart from Eric's. What was normal and right for her was a foreign language to him. For instance, when Eric didn't approach her sexually, she did what seemed natural to her: She tried to talk to him about it. For Eric, this was the wrong approach. He experienced it as a verbal barrage. What he needed was quiet action, such as he had seen his mother do for his father.

Eric was already feeling overwhelmed at work, and the last thing he wanted was to feel pressure at home. His company was recently purchased by a large conglomerate, and he felt under the gun to perform. Whereas work had never affected his sex drive before, this was not the case at midlife.

Now when he came home tired and worried, he didn't feel like staying up late, and he wasn't "up" for sex either. He wanted quiet understanding, gentle companionship, and even mild affection. But he needed it all to be low key.

As Hillary began to understand Eric's needs at this midlife juncture, she approached him in a language he was able to comprehend. Eric, for his part, learned to appreciate his wife's desire for physical and verbal connection, rather than misinterpret it as an effort to control him.

The key for this couple was to realize that how each saw the marriage was neither right nor wrong, just different, and that both perspectives were valid. Once they understood and accepted the value of both viewpoints, they were able to resolve their differences more effectively.

✹

**Your family of origin colors what feels normal, comfortable,
and right in your marriage at midlife. To reduce conflict,
try to see issues through the looking glass of
your partner's point of view.**

✹

## Family Myth #2: My Partner Will Make Me Whole

Ross was a man's man, but when he fell for a woman, he fell hard and deep. Such was the case with his second wife Angie. All had gone well for the first ten years of their marriage, until Angie hit forty and decided to go to law school. Things went from bad to worse later that year when Ross hurt his back at work and was put on permanent disability after twenty-two years on the job as a firefighter.

He was referred by his physician for depression when he became suicidal after Angie threatened to leave him. She drove him to his first appointment. "I can't take it anymore," she complained. "He's driving me crazy. He won't let me out of his sight. I love him, but he's got to give me room to breathe."

Ross was furious. "How could she even think of abandoning me now!" He winced in pain as he straightened his back and continued. "I love her more than anything in the world," he added, his voice a mixture of sadness and anger. "Since her son moved out, she's hardly home anymore. What about me?"

Over the next few weeks, Ross came in for individual therapy, since Angie was too busy with finals. It provided good grist for the mill. "She can't even find time for this," he barked. But Angie's absence gave breathing room for us to explore some old wounds that had resurfaced.

## DON'T PROJECT UNMET NEEDS FROM
## YOUR PAST ONTO YOUR PARTNER

Ross had a reservoir of unresolved grief related to his mother's gradual death from multiple sclerosis. He was ten when she died, but he had lost pieces of her year by year ever since he was born, as the disease progressively sapped her ability to care for her two sons. His older brother went away to prep school soon after she died, leaving Ross alone with his grief-stricken father, who withdrew into work to cope with his sadness.

Ross had reason to feel abandoned in the present, but these early losses compounded his unconscious reaction to his wife's newfound independence. Even Angie's son moving out when she went to law school matched Ross's sense of loss when his brother went away shortly after his mother died.

He felt totally abandoned, and it devastated him. Rather than deal with his pain, he frantically reached for Angie like an overboard sailor lunges for a lifesaver. The harder he grasped, the more she pushed away. Psychologically, he expected his wife to fill the hole left after his mom died. Angie's newfound independence at midlife unconsciously reminded him of his early loss.

This is not uncommon, but even if you don't have such dramatic unfinished business left over from childhood, those early years can create areas of sensitivity when it comes to your ongoing intimate relationship. They're often at the root of your deepest longings and sharpest disappointments.

❋

**Don't expect your partner to complete or make you whole, especially at painful midlife junctures. It's not your spouse's job to become your loving parent.**

❋

## CHANGE YOURSELF RATHER THAN YOUR PARTNER

Nor is it your job to change your partner either. Angie learned that the hard way. It's one of the reasons she shifted direction so dramatically when she hit forty. After ten years of either placating Ross's needy "little boy" or trying to convince him to loosen his grip and allow her more independence, she decided to change herself instead.

That didn't happen overnight, however. Angie grew up watching her father dominate her mother, so her marital models were of a woman appeasing her husband at every turn. Angie learned from her parents that it was a wife's duty to "honor and obey." She faithfully followed that model during early adulthood, but at midlife, sensing time running out, she decided to follow her own dreams rather than her husband's.

This was a wise decision, although not an easy one, and not without its share of conflict. But as we often tell couples, you can't decide whether your partner will change, but you can take charge of your own behavior. Because you've got more control there, you're more likely to transform your relationship. Rather than passively bemoan your spouse's limitations or be run ragged by them, it's healthier mentally to face them squarely and to change yourself accordingly.

＊

**Don't expect to change your partner. If you want to rewrite the rules of your relationship at midlife, you're more likely to be successful changing yourself.**

＊

Ross and Angie eventually renegotiated a new relationship at midlife. One of the keys was Angie having the courage and strength to grow beyond the marital models she witnessed during childhood. It was also important for Ross to let go of some of his old, unmet needs from childhood as well. Once these unconscious family myths were brought up into the daylight, their power was considerably reduced.

To recap, cultural and family myths can set you up with false expectations about marriage at midlife. The more you become aware of these unrealistic assumptions, the less likely you are to be dissatisfied with your relationship. In chapter 4 you'll learn ways to change these dysfunctional beliefs into more realistic ways of thinking about your marriage, a key way to increase marital satisfaction.

### CHAPTER 4

# Change Your Relationship by Changing Yourself

*Most folks are as happy as they make up their minds to be.*
—Abraham Lincoln

Roberta saw her husband's eyes scan more than the menu at the local steak house. As far as she was concerned, the dish he was drooling over was a young waitress in a short skirt. Her face flushed with rage as she abruptly slammed down her menu and angrily grabbed her purse. Their twentieth-anniversary dinner was over before it began.

"How could you do this to me," she asked, the venom in her voice more an indictment than a question. "You know it hurts my feelings, yet you continue to gawk at every young thing that walks by in a dress. I've had it!" She pushed her chair back with a loud screech, snatched up her sweater, and headed for the door.

Her husband, Rolland, was crestfallen. He had even taken off his glasses as soon as they sat down, hoping Roberta wouldn't think he was looking at other women. He loved his wife, but his patience was wearing thin. Since she turned forty the previous year, Roberta frequently went ballistic with her jealous rages. The scene at the restaurant was the final straw for Rolland. He called us the following morning for an appointment.

What soon became apparent was Roberta's sensitivity to distrust. She came by it honestly, for her stepfather cheated on her mother and was sexually suggestive with Roberta as well. Those experiences during adolescence had left a scar on Roberta's psyche; she became hesitant to trust men and wary of being betrayed by them. A key part of marital therapy was teaching Roberta how to challenge her faulty assumptions about the present and then to reinterpret them more realistically.

As we mentioned in the previous chapter, the culture and your family of origin can predispose you, like Roberta, to certain unrealistic expectations about your relationship. Now it's time to learn how to catch those mistakes before they blossom into dissatisfaction, frustration, and conflict. Such positive "self-talk," being realistic when you talk to yourself about your relationship experiences and expectations, can significantly increase your marital satisfaction.

❋

**How you interpret marital experiences, the meaning you give to them, directly affects your marital satisfaction. The good news is that you can learn to talk to yourself more realistically.**

❋

Roberta had another battle to fight with her past. Her mother had drilled her repeatedly with how important it was for a girl to be pretty. It was the cornerstone of who Roberta was as a person. Her brilliant legal career, her position as state president of a prestigious organization, and her national awards as a college debater all paled in significance, as far as Roberta was concerned. Her mother's mantra (as well as the culture's) was always front and center: If she wasn't physically attractive, she wasn't worth much.

As a younger woman, she felt confident. She was a shapely brunette with long legs and a beautiful face. But when she hit forty, she became frantic. She had her face done, enrolled in several diet programs and two gyms in the course of four months, and exercised for at least an hour every morning. She was still beautiful, especially to Rolland, but you couldn't convince Roberta of that.

"I was always being compared to my cousin Belinda," she told us. "Mom's high school sweetheart dumped my mom and married my aunt Maria, her younger sister. She was prettier than Mom, and Mom was determined to even the score."

Roberta's eyes moistened as she took a slow breath and sighed. "So I had to be better than my cousin, especially prettier, but I always came in second. Even when I became a homecoming princess, Belinda was voted homecoming queen. Mom still compares us," Roberta continued. "It's crazy."

## Be Careful Whom You Compare Yourself to at Midlife

Mom wasn't the only one doing the comparing. Unconsciously, Roberta compared herself with every woman who crossed her path, and especially those who crossed Rolland's path. As beautiful as she was, there were always other women who were more attractive. Because of her past experiences with Belinda, Roberta tended to compare herself only with those who were prettier than she was. She rarely compared herself with the 90 percent who weren't as attractive.

That, according to the research, can bring you down psychologically. For instance, when researchers looked at Olympic silver and bronze medalists, they noticed a curious thing. The silver medalists, even though they had outperformed those who won the bronze, felt less satisfied with themselves. Why? Well, how happy you are, according to the researchers, depends on who you compare yourself to. The silver medalists felt like failures because they were so close to winning it all, but didn't. Their self-talk was negative: "Another inch and I would have been the best in the world."

The bronze medalists, on the other hand, said things to themselves like, "Well, at least I won a medal as opposed to being just one of the field," so they were more satisfied. Compared to the other athletes who competed and had nothing to show for it, those who won the bronze were thrilled to stand on the podium and represent their countries.[1]

Like the Olympic medalists, Roberta's problem wasn't how attractive she was, but who she compared herself to. A key trigger for her was allowing her attention to linger on the beautiful women who would occasionally come into her field of vision. Choosing to focus exclusively on them inevitably triggered a cascade of self-torment. When she learned to positively compare herself to the many women who weren't as attractive as she was, it boosted her self-esteem and lessened her marital conflict.

*

**Beware of whom you compare yourself to at midlife.**
**That can trigger a negative appraisal of yourself**
**or your relationship.**

*

*This is certainly true in our relationship. If I compared Steve to other husbands when it comes to helping out around the house, our marriage would be in trouble. On a scale of one to ten, he's probably a two, on good days. Maybe we shouldn't admit this in print, but he even bought me a pipe wrench for Mother's Day one year.*

*I could misinterpret Steve's poor showing in this department as a lack of caring or love for me. But when I'm realistic with my self-talk, I know not to take this shortcoming of his personally. I also remind myself of the numerous other ways he does show his love, many of which are the envy of my friends.*

*He loves to dance with me, has been an involved father and a successful provider, and frequently tells me how lucky he is to have me as his wife. So I try to see his deficiency in this one area for what it is: a weakness of his rather than a commentary about my self-worth or his love for me.*

## Talk to Yourself More Positively

Essentially, self-talk is a four-step process. First, something triggers you to react. In Roberta's case, it was crossing paths with attractive women when she was with her husband. The key here is to become more aware of what triggers you at midlife and to develop an action plan ahead of time.

Step two is the faulty assumption or conclusion you come to about the trigger event, like Roberta's mistaken interpretation of what it meant when her husband glanced at a young waitress. Roberta needed to see it for what it was: a normal response by a heterosexual male. Although the behavior was his, the meaning she gave to it was hers. As the poet Gary Snyder wrote: "Our immediate business, and our quarrel, is with ourselves."[2]

Step three is the consequence on your relationship when you leap to a faulty conclusion. With Roberta and Rolland, it invariably resulted in the same old argument. Depression, conflict, and divorce are common consequences for midlife couples when they jump on similar merry-go-rounds.

Step four is where you prevent faulty assumptions from derailing your relationship at midlife. We'll show you how to reinterpret your negative self-talk, avoid taking control issues too personally, and allow your spouse to be separate and different. You'll also learn how to prepare positive reinterpretations ahead of time, sensibly divert and distract yourself, and use spirituality (if you're so inclined) to change your mind-set as well.

❋

**In the four steps of negative self-talk,**
**(1)** *midlife triggers* **set off (2)** *faulty assumptions,* **resulting in**
**(3)** *marital consequences,* **but you can learn to**
**(4)** *reinterpret them effectively.*

❋

## Reinterpret Negative Self-Talk

The best way to beat negative self-talk is to learn how to realistically and positively reinterpret your midlife triggers. This was critical for Lauren and her husband, Mitch, after Lauren opened up a daycare facility in their home once the youngest of their three children started full-time at school. Mitch complained constantly that the house was always a mess, and Lauren would run around frantically trying to straighten it up before he came home in the evening.

When she first came to see us, it was for depression. But it quickly became apparent that she was angry at her husband. "He's always criticizing me," she said quietly. "I don't know if I can take it much longer."

Earlier in the marriage, Lauren had been content to let Mitch set the tone and take the lead in their relationship. Now, at thirty-eight, she was becoming more her own person, emotionally and financially. The success of her marriage depended on how successfully she and her husband navigated her midlife transition.

"My life feels like a sequence of chapters in a novel," she continued, describing her journey through motherhood. "Mitch is more like an arrow shot from a strong bow; his direction never waivers." Lauren's creative description applies to most men and women.

For Mitch's identity was firmly attached to his success as a provider and his career with the phone company. Lauren's, however, changed dramatically when she had three children in the course of five years.

Now it was changing again as her youngest went off to school and she began a new career. Her newfound freedom reflected the budding autonomy of her children. Lauren needed a new relationship to house her emerging independent identity.

*

**Many wives experience life as a sequence of chapters in a book, as children are born, mature, and eventually leave the nest. Men are more like arrows on a mission that waivers little.**

*

Consistent with his mission, Mitch was reluctant to change, at least not without some prodding. Although he loved his wife and was a loyal and hardworking husband and father, he was the kind of guy you needed to hit on the head with a two-by-four to get his attention.

Some of this was due to his adult attention deficit disorder, which distracted him and caused him to talk excessively and to interrupt Lauren impulsively. He meant well, but he had great difficulty seeing beyond his own thoughts and opinions.

His lengthy analyses and lectures were hard to derail once he got rolling.

He also operated on some traditional expectations about the roles husbands and wives should play in a relationship. He genuinely believed that it was his job to "teach" his wife about life, although this was partly because he was ten years older. Lauren accepted her conservative position within the marriage for the most part. She, more than Mitch, was a faithful member of a fundamentalist Christian church.

But his unconscious assumption that his opinions and reasoning were somehow more substantial than hers increasingly rubbed her the wrong way as she grew older. She felt discounted and insignificant, especially when he interrupted her after barely listening to what she had to say.

The good news and the bad news for Mitch, however, was that Lauren was learning to assert herself. The bad news, as far as Mitch was concerned, was that after fifteen relatively quiet years of marriage, his wife was now rocking the marital boat. What Mitch needed to learn was that it was actually good news, for if she didn't assert herself, she would eventually leave him.

The more passive Lauren was in the relationship, the more depressed and resentful she became. When she withdrew, Mitch became anxious and filled the marital void by talking more, further overwhelming Lauren. It was an escalating cycle, and they both needed to become more aware of the roles they played perpetuating it.

As is not uncommon, those roles were based on negative or inaccurate self-talk. A key part of helping this couple through this dangerous midlife transition was teaching them how to look at each other and themselves differently. Once they were able to reinterpret key trigger points more constructively, they were then able to make the necessary changes in their relationship.

For instance, Mitch "catastrophized" or "awfulized" about what was actually healthy marital communication. As soon as Lauren voiced any disagreement or dissatisfaction, he leapt to the faulty conclusion that this was a challenge to his authority in the relationship.

Even more concerning to Mitch was his fear that she would leave him. Underneath his macho, lecturing style, Mitch worried that Lauren would abandon him like his first wife did, a divorce that had left him suicidal and severely depressed for over a year.

He needed to nip this misinterpretation in the bud and rationally reinterpret what it meant when Lauren shared her disappointment with him. It took him several months, but he grew to realize that listening to his wife actually enhanced the security he was afraid of losing at midlife.

❋

**Rather than "catastrophize" or "awfulize" about your partner or your relationship at midlife, change how you feel by reinterpreting key midlife trigger points.**

❋

*Learn the Four Steps to Reinterpret Negative Self-Talk*

Here's a summary of how Mitch changed his negative self-talk. Become familiar with the four steps. You'll have an opportunity later to use them on *your* midlife relationship.

- *Step 1—Midlife Trigger:* As far as Mitch was concerned, the trigger for their marital conflict was when Lauren complained or argued with him. This was new behavior for her, and Mitch wasn't used to it. It reflected her growth as an individual during her middle years. It was also an effort on her part to beat back her depression and save her marriage.

- *Step 2—Faulty Assumption:* Mitch misinterpreted the trigger of Lauren's newfound assertiveness in two ways. First, he discounted her opinions and dismissed her feelings as insignificant. That faulty assumption was partly due to his attention deficit disorder, but his traditional gender conditioning also added to the problem. Second, he incorrectly worried that her opposition meant that the relationship was in trouble, for she hadn't complained much in the past when he corrected her or took a leadership role in the relationship.

- *Step 3—Relationship Consequence:* His misinterpretations had serious marital consequences. When Mitch discounted Lauren's feelings, she grew more depressed and distant. Also, when he mistook her assertiveness for conflict, he became anxious and even more determined to convince Lauren of the wisdom of his position. His intensified lectures further overwhelmed and frustrated her.

- *Step 4—Realistic Reinterpretation:* Mitch learned to reinterpret Lauren's "opposition" as her asserting her point of view and not as a direct challenge to him. He grew to realize that this was healthier for their relationship than her repressing her feelings and then growing depressed and distant. He also learned to listen and to value Lauren's perspective, rather than belittle or dismiss it.

Lauren also had considerable work to do rethinking her assumptions about the marriage. One of the biggest was overcoming her hesitation to speak up for herself. This was partly due to her socialization as a female, especially coming from a family that thought of women as second-class citizens.

Her father was an old-world rancher who ruled with an iron fist. Lauren spent most of her childhood peeking out from behind her mother's apron while watching her mom cower and cater. She was terrified of her father, and when she married a man ten years her senior, she picked up where she left off: being the obedient little girl.

Midlife changed all that. With the last of her three children off to school and a thriving business all her own, Lauren felt like "somebody" for the first time in her life. She wasn't the same obedient little girl Mitch had married fifteen years earlier, but she didn't know how to assert herself, either. It was a foreign language, especially coming from her background.

Before she could assert herself with Mitch, she had to redefine who she was and what she could expect from a marriage. In short, she needed to change how she talked to herself before she could talk to her husband differently. Here's a brief overview of the four steps Lauren took to change her negative self-talk.

- *Step 1—Midlife Trigger:* The key trigger for Lauren was when Mitch lectured or criticized her, especially about how messy the house was.
- *Step 2—Faulty Assumption:* She assumed that she had no right to disagree with him.
- *Step 3—Relationship Consequence:* Her assumed powerlessness led, as it often does, to depression and withdrawal from her husband.

• *Step 4—Realistic Reinterpretation:* Once she owned her own power, she learned how to assert herself and redefined her marriage at midlife.

To identify your midlife triggers, pay attention to those issues that recur periodically in your relationship. For Lauren, it was her husband's criticism. Then examine how you talk to yourself about those triggers and challenge your assumptions.

❋

**Identify midlife triggers that set you off and become more aware of your faulty assumptions. When you realistically reinterpret what triggers you, your relationship changes.**

❋

*When Steve didn't do the shopping yesterday, how I talked to myself definitely affected our relationship. Here's a summary of the four steps I took to alter my negative self-talk.*

• Step 1—Midlife Trigger: *He chose to write rather than go shopping, focusing on his needs rather than the family's.*
• Step 2—Faulty Assumption: *"He never pulls his weight. I do everything around here."*
• Step 3—Relationship Consequence: *I start to get angry and anticipate letting him have it when I get home, but then I remember to "do the four-step," as we jokingly refer to it in our marital workshops.*
• Step 4—Realistic Reinterpretation: *"He's struggling with chapter five, not lying on the couch watching football. True, I do more on the domestic front, but he's putting in more hours on the book, so it balances out for now."*

*It's important to be honest with yourself, however. This reinterpretation worked for me, but it might not work for you. In this case, once I talked to myself differently, I was able to let it go.*

*If it hadn't worked, I would have needed to move from self-talk to partner-talk, which we'll get into in the next few chapters. Remember: Blocked feelings create distance. If self-talk changes things, great. But if it doesn't, don't eat crow. You and your relationship will ultimately pay the price in distance and resentment.*

### Don't Take Control Issues Too Personally

It's also important not to take things personally, as in the earlier example with Lauren and Mitch. Besides Lauren feeling criticized and lectured to about how messy the house was, she also felt Mitch was trying to control her.

This is a common faulty assumption in an ongoing intimate relationship. But it's also a dangerous one. It's important to reinterpret such a trigger, for if you see your spouse as striving to control you, you're more likely to become defensive and argumentative.

• *Step 1—Midlife Trigger:* When Mitch lectured Lauren about how to keep the house clean.

• *Step 2—Faulty Assumption:* "He's just trying to control me. He loves to tell me what to do!"

• *Step 3—Relationship Consequence:* Lauren typically withdrew in angry silence. Mitch would then get nervous and try to explain his position in greater detail. This would further overwhelm Lauren, who would get even angrier and leave the house. Instead, she used step 4.

• *Step 4—Realistic Reinterpretation:* "He's a 'neat freak,' and I'm not. Perhaps if we talk it over, we can come to a compromise."

The key here is that Lauren catches her faulty assumption and reinterprets her husband's behavior more realistically. They still have their differences, but she's not taking it personally.

As the Gestalt psychiatrist Fritz Perls once said, "Contact is the appreciation of differences." While Lauren's probably not "appreciating" those differences, and who could blame her, she's not overreacting and falsely projecting an extra layer of malevolent intent onto her husband.

It's true that "even paranoids have real enemies," as one political button during the '60s read, and that sometimes spouses attempt to control for control's sake. But it's far more likely that your partner is just scrambling about, trying to get his or her needs met. Beware of taking it too personally and projecting more onto it than is intended.

With control issues, rationally sift through how your partner's behavior impacts on you. Then try to see it as your spouse intended it. If you can do those two things, you'll be well on your way to a more realistic reinterpretation of a potentially troubling marital trigger and a more likely resolution to a possible conflict.

❊

**Don't take marital differences too personally. Odds are your partner is just struggling to get his or her needs met and not intentionally trying to control you.**

❊

## ALLOW YOUR SPOUSE TO BE
## SEPARATE AND DIFFERENT

One of the problems with Mitch and Lauren was Mitch's insistence that his wife do things his way. It's not that he was a tyrant. He was just totally unaware that Lauren perceived and accomplished things differently from the way he did.

This is partly due to the "I'm Right, You're Wrong" myth of the previous chapter. Remember how the artist, environmentalist, and real estate developer all saw something entirely different when they looked at the same strip of California coastline? Well, Mitch and Lauren, and you and your partner, for that matter, often see and value things just as differently.

Whether it's your child-rearing philosophies, sexual appetites, spending habits, or personal definitions of neat and tidy, you and your spouse are each unique in hundreds of important and distinct ways. You presumably respect those discrepancies with friends. Why not extend the same courtesy to your mate?

When you began your relationship, you probably experienced your partner's uniqueness as entertaining, stimulating, or intriguing. At the very least, many of his or her idiosyncrasies were barely blips on your radar screen.

For example, Mitch found Lauren's carefree attitude refreshing at first, and during the early stages of their relationship he hardly noticed when she left magazines or mail on the kitchen table. But over the years he unconsciously expected her to become more like him, and he was obsessive-compulsive when it came to neatness.

Her change at midlife threw him over the edge. Whereas previously she was willing to placate his sense of orderliness, she needed more latitude now that she had a business to run. At thirty-eight, she was also tired of playing the "obedient little girl."

This was extremely difficult for Mitch, as it is for many spouses during their middle years. Besides struggling to accommodate a wife at midlife who was pushing for more independence, he was not a flexible man to begin with, and flexibility is a core ingredient for a successful relationship at any stage.

Still, he showed progress rewriting the inner script of his unproductive self-talk. This was instrumental in saving his marriage and renewing his relationship at midlife.

• *Step 1—Midlife Trigger:* Mitch's main trigger was when he walked through the den and patio where Lauren operated her child-care facility.

• *Step 2—Faulty Assumptions:*

1. "How could she be so disorganized! I'd never leave a workplace looking like that."

2. "I can't stand the mess. It's intolerable."

3. "If I don't straighten her out, she'll keep making the same mistake."

• *Step 3—Relationship Consequence:* Whenever Mitch criticized Lauren for not picking up more thoroughly, she resentfully withdrew, and marital distance resulted. Instead, he effectively reinterprets their differences in step 4.

• *Step 4—Realistic Reinterpretations:*

1. "She leaves her work area messier than I would, but I must remember that she's different from me. She has a looser sense of organization, and sometimes that's not so bad."

2. "Her schoolrooms are off to the side, so if I don't open the door, it won't bother me as much. It's not 'intolerable.'"

3. "I can't expect her to do things my way. If I try to push my sense of neatness and order onto her, she'll only resent me for it, and our marriage will suffer. I need to give her room as a separate person."

Mitch changed his self-talk in three key ways. First he allowed Lauren to be Lauren rather than expecting her to have the same sense of organization he did. Second, he no longer "awfulized" about the problem. It was *not* intolerable. And he even came up with the creative solution of not opening the door to her classrooms. Out of sight, out of mind is good psychology. Third, he gave her space to be a separate individual, rather than trying to mold her into a clone of himself.

❋

**Don't push your spouse to think or behave like you do.**
**Allow differences. Give partners more space to be**
**separate and independent at midlife as well.**
**They often demand it.**

❋

## PREPARE POSITIVE REINTERPRETATIONS AHEAD OF TIME

Another way to change how you think and feel about your relationship at midlife is to arm yourself in advance before trouble begins. This was especially helpful for Bonnie in her twenty-year marriage with Byron, a workaholic and self-centered surgeon. You can use this technique not only to strengthen how you perceive your relationship, but to boost how you feel about yourself as well.

Bonnie needed both. She had terrible self-esteem, and she badly misinterpreted Byron's selfishness and need for recognition in the community as meaning he didn't love her. So when he put in extra hours on hospital committees and medical boards, she would misinterpret that as meaning she was stupid and uninteresting, both old messages she received during childhood.

Bonnie prepared to combat those old messages with three honest positives, which she came up with and wrote on a card to keep in her wallet. Then, when a trigger hit and she would begin to assume the worst, she had three weapons on hand to help defeat her negative self-talk.

Those three positives served as Bonnie's pre-rehearsed, realistic reinterpretations. Because step 4 is often hard to do in the midst of battle, preparing ahead of time can give you a leg up on your negative self-talk.

- *Step 1—Midlife Trigger:* Byron calls from the office to tell her to hold dinner; he'll be half an hour late.
- *Step 2—Faulty Assumption:* "He doesn't care about me. Why should he? I'm pretty boring and not very smart."
- *Step 3—Relationship Consequence:* Bonnie is about to withdraw into her bedroom after dinner to read by herself, but instead she tries step 4.
- *Step 4—Realistic Reinterpretations (Three Honest Positives):*

    1. "All the customers at work always ask for me rather than Debbie or Gail."
    2. "My three children are all successful, popular, and happy."
    3. "Byron wrote me a beautiful poem on our twentieth anniversary and insisted on a big remarriage ceremony at the church."

Those were three powerful positives, and they worked. Bonnie reflected on her list for a few minutes while drying the dishes. She even added an extra positive, that Byron was washing the dishes right next to her, as he usually did after dinner. Instead of slinking off by herself to the bedroom as she might have done in times past, Bonnie and Byron watched a romantic movie and then sailed off to the bedroom together to make love.

Bonnie's problem in the past was that although she had a lot going for her, it often got drowned out by the negative voices of her childhood. Once they were triggered, they were difficult to quiet. Her list of positives helped. They were instruments of reason not easily overcome by the clamor of childhood memories.

Those three positives were all true; Bonnie just needed to be reminded of them. At work, she was the most sought after legal secretary in the office. Clients trusted her judgment, and she was always cheerful and willing to help.

Also, all three of her adolescent and adult children were doing exceptionally well: no minor accomplishment, especially in this day and age. She had succeeded at what she considered her primary job, being a mom.

Finally, when she talked rationally to herself, she realized that her husband did indeed value and love her. True, he was a self-centered workaholic, but it wasn't Bonnie's fault. His poem was in fact quite flattering and strongly endorsed how much she meant to him.

Bonnie's three honest positives contained two individual affirmations and one relationship example. You be the judge of what mix is best for you. If you tend to be low in self-esteem, your examples don't necessarily need to be marital. They should counter your most likely faulty assumption, however, and they should be significant and honest positives. Don't tell us you don't have any. Everybody has gifts and talents; you just need to search for them.

If your self-esteem isn't in question, pick three positives about your relationship or your partner. For instance, Bonnie could have reminded herself that Byron never cheated on her, always remembered her birthday and anniversaries, and was a steady provider and father. He also loved her about as much as he could love anybody other than himself.

It took her a while before she was able to employ her three positives effectively. Even then, they didn't work all the time. But after several weeks, she became more adept at pulling out her card and forcefully talking to herself more positively. It's not easy to catch your negative self-talk. But with practice and perseverance, it can be done, and it can significantly renew your marriage at midlife.

✷

**Keep a list of three honest positives about yourself, your partner, or your relationship in your wallet. You'll be better prepared to beat back negative self-talk when it strikes.**

✷

Now you try it. You don't have much to lose, and it only takes five minutes. List three honest positives about yourself, your spouse, or your marriage. Then put them either in your wallet, over your desk at work, in the car, or in several places so they're readily accessible.

When a midlife trigger hits, you'll be better prepared to dispute your negative beliefs or assumptions. This won't always work, and it will probably take some practice before you become skilled at effectively beating back your negative self-talk. But it's a debate you need to learn how to win, for your emotional and marital reality is mostly an inside job.

## DIVERT AND DISTRACT YOURSELF

Besides disrupting your negative self-talk, studies show that it helps to divert or distract yourself as well. The research also reveals that it's a strategy more likely to be used by men than women. This was the case with Byron and Bonnie, and was especially helpful to him when she would try to discipline their last remaining child at home, sixteen-year-old Amanda.

Bonnie's gentle and permissive parenting style drove Byron

crazy. "If I don't leave the room, I'll either say something or have a coronary," he said with great irritation. The surgeon had a point. Remember, out of sight, out of mind is good psychology, especially before your self-talking gathers momentum. By diverting his attention, he saved his marriage a good deal of unnecessary conflict.

- *Step 1—Midlife Trigger:* Bonnie is too soft disciplining their teenage daughter, as far as Byron is concerned.
- *Step 2—Faulty Assumption:* "She doesn't know how to discipline kids. I should go in there and straighten things out."
- *Step 3—Relationship Consequence:* Whenever Byron interferes, Bonnie typically gets angry and storms out of the room.
- *Step 4—Diversion & Distraction:* Instead, Byron diverts his attention by withdrawing into another room, thereby saving a marital conflict.

Although the last step is somewhat different, this variation of the four-step process is still an effective way to prevent negative self-talk from disrupting a relationship. In this case, rather than reinterpret his faulty assumptions, Byron circumvents a potential conflict by diverting or distracting himself.

Exercise is another way to divert or distract yourself, plus the endorphins you release into your bloodstream won't hurt your marital disposition either. Just a five-minute walk around the block gives you enough time to collect yourself emotionally.

Spending time with friends, even a quick phone call, is also a good diversion. Research shows that this is a common strategy for women and tends to reduce stress, which would likely contribute to lessening marital conflict as well. Activities such as going to the movies or reading will also do the trick.

One warning to keep in mind, however: Beware of diverting and distracting yourself to the point of avoidance. You don't want to sweep so many issues under the rug that you're left with a huge mound in the middle of the room for you and your partner to trip over. Use as a spice, not as a main ingredient. If you can combine diverting and distracting with realistic reinterpretation, all the better. Sometimes, however, that's just too difficult to pull off.

*My favorite diversionary tactic is knitting. When I started to edit some of Steve's work on chapter two, I could tell by his tone and the way he tightened his lips that he was getting uptight. When he angled the computer screen away from me and toward him, I knew we were in for a battle. How ironic: The two relationship experts about to go at it over the text of their marital self-help book!*

*I felt annoyed when he moved the screen away. I was beginning to build up a head of steam myself, when I reinterpreted my faulty assumption that he was trying to control me. I remembered that he generally likes more time to process things than I do, and that although his period of analysis is paralysis for me, it prevents him from feeling overwhelmed and out of control.*

*So I took a little of our own medicine and "did the four-step." When I reinterpreted this potential control trigger, I was able to see it as Steve's problem, and gave him the space he needed to process my feedback without him feeling over-*

*whelmed by me. I also pulled out my knitting. It diverted my attention and helped me cool down. I was then able to wait more patiently.*

- Step 1—Midlife Trigger: *Steve gets tense, slows down, and seeks control.*
- Step 2—Faulty Assumption: *"He's got some nerve. Turning the screen away was downright rude! He has no right to treat me like that."*
- Step 3—Relationship Consequence: *I'm about to let him have it, whereupon he would have gotten defensive, and we would have had to use our communication skills (the ones we'll show you in the next three chapters) to dig ourselves out. Instead, I moved to step 4.*
- Step 4—Realistic Reinterpretation + Diversion & Distraction:

*1. "Steve's getting uptight because he needs time to process the feedback I'm giving him. His move with the screen was just an oblique signal to me. If I back off and go slower, he'll calm down."*

*2. I take out my knitting to distract myself. This helps divert my energy and calms me down. Because I'm less overwhelming, Steve doesn't need to push me away, and we prevent a potential control struggle.*

*The combination of reinterpreting Steve's behavior and diverting myself with my knitting worked. The key here was not biting the hook, or at least getting myself unhooked early enough in the process. We were then able to move ahead, even finding something positive out of the experience, for it did provide us with this instructive example.*

           ❋

**Learn to divert and distract yourself. Exercise, social support, and other activities can help defuse tension and prevent conflict. Don't overdo it, however, to the point of avoidance.**

           ❋

### CONSIDER SPIRITUAL SELF-TALK

There is a story of a young nun who goes to the mother superior and says, "Mother, I am so stressed. I have so many commitments and obligations. What should I do?"

And the mother superior says, "Well, then pray, my child." But the young nun is not so easily convinced. She presses on in great detail about her stress and woe.

"But Mother, you don't understand," she adds in great agitation. "I don't have time to pray."

To which the mother superior replies, "Well, in that case, my child, pray double."

There is much wisdom in that story, and to the spiritual path in general. For it is at just such times of stress and turmoil that we most need to center ourselves, to meditate, or to pray.

Spirituality is a sensitive subject, and we don't mean to imply that you should practice or study a particular path or religion. But the bottom line psychologically is that spirituality is a time-honored, cross-cultural way to quiet the mind and cope with stress.

After all, Psyche, whose name is the root of the word *psychology*, was the Greek goddess of the soul or spirit. Spirituality is essentially self-talk, with a capital S for one's higher, spiritual "Self" or soul.

For many, spirituality means praying to God. For others, it's getting in touch with Mother Nature. And for still others, it means a Higher Power, Great Spirit, or even the Force from the *Star Wars* movies. But however you do it, get in touch with that "still small voice" within, for meditation can be powerful medication for relationship stress and conflict.

This can be especially true at midlife, when we begin to put things more earnestly into a larger "perspective." A spiritual perspective proved to be Bonnie's best game plan in her marriage with Byron. Whereas Byron used diversion and distraction to cope with marital stress, Bonnie went to Mass. Her Catholic upbringing didn't do much for her self-esteem when she was young, but it was powerful medicine in her fight against loneliness and despair during her middle years. She put it to good use one weekend in her four-step battle against her negative self-talk.

- *Step 1—Midlife Trigger:* None of her kids called for several weekends, and Byron worked all day Saturday and did paperwork that Sunday.
- *Step 2—Faulty Assumption:* "Nobody cares about me. I'm pretty unimportant. Actually, worthless is probably more like it!"
- *Step 3—Relationship Consequence:* Bonnie began to snipe at Byron, driving him even further away. Then she did her four-step, which, for her, was prayer.
- *Step 4—Spiritual Reinterpretation:* Bonnie experienced

connecting with God during Sunday Mass and left feeling less lonely and unloved.

Prayer didn't always work for her, but she frequently felt spiritually centered and rejuvenated after Mass, and that soothed her key midlife trigger—loneliness—especially with her exiting children and workaholic husband. "It's as if I lose myself in God," she reflected, "and all my petty problems are seen in a new light."

Although Bonnie turned to religion, many at midlife look to nature. For instance, we often walk down our country road and marvel at heron as they glide low over the creek or the setting sun's light as it radiates neighboring sycamore and oak.

There is a Jewish prayer on Hanukkah that highlights the importance of being connected with such natural miracles of the moment. "Days pass and years vanish," it warns, "yet we walk sightless among miracles." When you're spiritually centered, relationship triggers become less overwhelming, and you're able to appreciate those miracles.

Thoreau in *Walden* used a different metaphor when he observed that "like the lake, my serenity is rippled but not ruffled." The trick is to quiet one's mind, to shut off the computer long enough to let God or Nature, or however it is you experience Spirit, to expand and breathe life into the silent spaces between your thoughts.

❋

**Spirituality can be good psychology and a powerful way to transcend relationship stress and loneliness. To experience midlife issues in a spiritual context is often to transform them.**

❋

The bottom line, whether it's through spiritual or more psychological reinterpretation of midlife triggers, is that you can change how you think about you, your partner, and your relationship. As you do, you literally re-create or renew your marriage.

# PART THREE

# Partner-Talk

*Negotiate Relationship
Differences*

✦

I will risk myself by endeavoring
to communicate any persistent
feeling, positive or negative,
to my partner. . . . Then I will risk
further by trying to understand,
with all the empathy I can bring
to bear, his or her response.

—Carl Rogers

### CHAPTER 5

# Listening to Changes at Midlife

Silence is one of the great arts of conversation.

—William Hazlitt

I called Cathy in to look at chapter 3. I felt uncertain about my writing and wondered if we could produce this book at all. She was encouraging enough, but then she began to take over the computer, editing as she went. As you may remember from the previous chapter, I tend to get uptight when she edits my work; this time was no exception.

She assumed that I would sit with her and keep her company while she read the first draft. That's not what I had in mind, however. I was excited about having the day to write and eager to get going. So I told her I wanted to get back to hitting the keys and asked her if she wouldn't mind editing later. Sounds simple enough, doesn't it? Well, as you know, nothing is simple when it comes to the relationship game. Anything can become a power struggle, and this one blew up in our faces.

Unlike the earlier example where Cathy pulled out her

*knitting and successfully "did the four-step," this time she angrily retreated to the dining room table and buried herself in the Saturday paper. I tried to get back to work, knowing full well that she was upset. But after staring vacantly at the computer screen, I realized that I wasn't going to create anything until we cleared this issue up.*

*So I took some of our own advice. I got up from the desk, walked into the dining room, pulled up a chair, and said, "I'm sorry. I know I upset you. Let me listen."*

So far we've focused on how you talk to yourself about your relationship at midlife. Now we look at how you talk to your partner.

Basically, communication is a two-way street. Picture yourself on one end of a telephone line and your partner on the other. You essentially need to do two things. First, you need to receive what your partner is sending. That's what this chapter is about: how to effectively listen to your spouse, especially when midlife change is afoot.

You also need to communicate your own desires. This can be particularly challenging if they've changed during your middle years. In the chapters that follow we'll show you how to meet your changing needs by attacking problems rather than your partner and how to put it all together to build a win-win relationship.

But the major midlife lesson is this: master how to listen. It is the single most important tool you can learn to prevent conflicts from erupting and to de-escalate them once they occur. The research is also encouraging. Studies show that these listening skills, as well as the other communication techniques we'll discuss, improve marital satisfaction and preserve relationships. In fact, we've conducted two studies on some of the hundreds of couples we've trained since 1975. Those who took the training significantly increased their level of marital satisfaction as well as their ability to communicate.

❋

**Studies of marital enrichment programs show that couples who learn to communicate increase their marital satisfaction and stay together longer than couples who don't learn these skills.**

❋

## Prepare to Listen

Try to read this paragraph while counting backward from 100 by fives. It's difficult to concentrate on two things at once, isn't it? You jump from one to the other, as your mind takes turns attending to either the next few words or a series of numbers. Here you have the luxury of pausing to reread a few words if you get lost. Your spouse won't be as generous if you miss a key point during a marital discussion, especially if he or she is upset about something. In order to listen effectively, you need to learn how to quiet your mind and focus your attention.

You probably quit counting backward from 100 and centered on what you were reading because your priority was learning how to help your relationship. Well, in a similar fashion, even before focusing your attention on your partner, you often need to choose whether you'll attend to your spouse or watch TV, make a business call, read the mail, or any number of competing demands. Just as you prioritized reading this page rather than doing the counting exercise, if you want to reduce conflict and improve your marriage, you need to make your relationship a priority.

The final step in preparing yourself before you can effectively listen is to quit doing the things that tend to backfire and irritate your partner, like giving advice or lecturing. Because they stop your spouse from sharing with you, we call them "Stoppers." By paying attention to your style of inattention, you can discover your particular brand of "Stopper." That, in itself, will pay big dividends when you and your partner have a difference of opinion.

❋

**Before you can effectively listen, you need to prepare yourself in three key ways: prioritize your relationship, quiet your mind, and stop saying or doing things that frustrate your partner.**

❋

### Prioritize the Relationship

Many couples fail to communicate because they don't make it a priority to begin with. This is especially common with listening and a chief stumbling block when you need to renew your relationship at midlife.

Your first mission, should you choose to become an effective listener, is to beat back your lethargy and your temptation to sweep your spouse's feelings and concerns under the rug. Listening can be a powerful tool to prevent dirt from building up under your relationship. But like vacuuming the rug, it doesn't happen by itself. You must decide to make it happen.

*Which is why I decided to get up and go into the dining room to listen to Cathy after I pushed her away when she tried to edit my writing. My listening began with a conscious decision to prioritize the relationship over the competing task of writing this book. Had I blocked out my awareness that Cathy was upset and just plowed on with the book, I would have been only half there anyway, and Cathy would have felt hurt and resentful that I not only rejected her, but didn't care enough to come talk to her about it.*

*The incident also would have added another brick in the always potentially growing wall of distance in our ongoing intimate relationship as a couple. We need to remove those bricks before the mortar that holds them together hardens. One of the best ways to do that is to prioritize your relationship; not just give lip service to the concept, but follow through on actually doing it, one incident at a time.*

*This is not easy, as we all know, for it means restraining ourselves from what seems like a more engaging or important activity, like in this case, my plan to eagerly get cracking on this book. But if I didn't choose to be flexible, to be aware of the needs of our relationship at that moment, we would have paid a price, albeit a small one for the time being. But add incidents like this up day*

*after day, year after year, and before you know it, you have a mar-*
*riage at midlife that's distant and near death.*

✵

**If you want to effectively listen, the first step is to make your**
**relationship the top priority, especially when your spouse is**
**upset. Avoid the temptation to sweep issues under the rug.**

✵

*Clear the Desktop:*
*Quiet the Mind and Put Down What You're Doing*

Did you ever suddenly lose yourself in a sunset, a starry sky, or
the sound of frogs or crickets on a summer night? When
it happens, it's a moment of magical clarity. Suddenly,
there's just you and the experience. Time feels like it's standing still.

Probably the most significant contributor to this marvelous
experience is the silence within your mind. For a brief moment, you stop talking to yourself. The usual chatter and clat-
ter of your thoughts are absent. You hear the frogs and crickets
because your thoughts aren't in the way.

Well, we don't mean to make it sound quite so mystical, but
listening to your partner begins with a similar clearing of the
"mind field." Or to use a computer metaphor, in order to listen, you must first clear the desktop of your mind. Once the
computer screen is empty, you're more open to receive new
information.

This is no easy task. Usually the mind is so full and busy,
you barely hear the crickets, let alone an angry spouse. When

your partner says things that frighten or annoy you, the computer screen rapidly fills up with defensive arguments and rebuttals. Your thoughts go into overdrive, and your ability to listen or take in your spouse's position is overwhelmed.

Keep clearing the desktop, however, for once your mind brims with rebuttal, your ability to empathize with your partner becomes severely limited. That, in turn, can escalate a spouse's frustration, sadness, and feelings of alienation and abandonment. It's bad enough to be hurt by the original incident. It's salt in the wounds to feel unheard or misunderstood when you're pouring your emotional guts out.

*It's easier to write about being open, harder to actually do it in real life, for it means being prepared to hear things you don't want to hear, things that sound wrong, trivial, irrelevant, or confrontational.*

*I was in for the latter, as Cathy let me have it: "You've been telling me what to do now for the last several days! Last night Kate told me that you said I couldn't help her with the school bond issue because we had a book to write. You also decided I shouldn't bid on some items at the preschool auction. Well, you don't make my decisions!"*

*She was on a roll now, and I knew that in order to get through this turn in the rapids, I had to hold on tight and go with the flow. So I took my own advice and just listened, keeping the computer screen empty. It was tempting to rebut what Cathy was saying, even if only in my mind, but I held course and kept my mouth shut and my mind open. I tried to take in and under-stand (stand under) what Cathy was saying. To feel what she was feeling, and how she had experienced these incidents, from her point of view.*

*She was telling me about herself, and I needed to listen, rather than take it personally. This wasn't about me; it was about Cathy's needs and feelings. Too often we overreact and personalize our spouse's comments, rather than tune into who our partner is and what he or she is sharing.*

*This is crucial, for had I clouded over in my own mind or begun to defend myself before she had gotten her position out on the table and heard, really listened to, the incident would surely have festered. She would have gotten angrier still, and then we'd have two problems on the burner: one, her feelings about my actions over the last few days, and two, her more immediate frustration and anger at me for not hearing her.*

*That second issue in many ways can be even more menacing to an ongoing intimate relationship, for it's happening right at the moment, and it feels like your partner doesn't care. It definitely adds a few bricks to that ever-threatening wall of resentment and distance—perhaps the single greatest danger to marriage at midlife.*

*So I held my tongue and kept an open mind.*

*It's important to remember that the journey can turn treacherous at any time, that it probably will when you hit relationship rapids, and that the best way to get through a turn of rough water is to get back to listening. That means prioritizing the relationship and quieting the mind. It also means recognizing key listening snafus that are likely to backfire and annoy your spouse.*

**You can't listen when you're busy defending or justifying your position. Your partner will sense you're not listening and that will increase conflict. Better to keep your mind open and alert.**

*Stop the "Stoppers": Don't Turn Off Your Partner*

You've now prioritized your relationship, cleared the "mind field," but perhaps you're still saying and doing things that drive your partner up the wall, like changing the subject too quickly, telling your spouse what to do about a problem, or belittling an issue. Well, join the crowd. All of us make blunders when we're listening, especially when our mate is angry or upset.

We call those mistakes Stoppers because besides irritating your partner, they also discourage or stop your partner from sharing further with you. This is no small matter. Remember: Distance is one of the greatest dangers facing a relationship at midlife.

There are three types of Stoppers. We've labeled them the "Three A's." Don't feel too badly if you find yourself committing several of them. Pay special attention to the one or two that you frequently use, your stock Stoppers. Getting a handle on them can be of tremendous value, especially when you and your spouse have an argument. Stopping your Stoppers won't further frustrate an already irritated partner, and you're far more likely then to resolve whatever conflict you're facing.

You're also more likely to avoid another common marital pitfall, annoying your partner simply by the way you listen, when maybe your spouse wasn't upset with you to begin with. How you listen to your mate when he or she is emotionally frustrated, even if the original subject had nothing to do with you, can *create* a problem between the two of you. If you "stop" your spouse midstream, you're likely to become the new target of frustration.

## STOPPERS: THE THREE A's

Altruistic Stoppers occur when you try too hard to be nice or helpful, like giving advice when your partner would rather have you listen. Advice when asked for is welcomed and even appreciated. "Why don't you forget about it and go for a walk," might work *after* your partner feels heard, but don't try that one too early in the game. Your partner can feel dismissed, invalidated, and unimportant.

### Altruistic Stoppers

Advising/Suggesting: "Try not to let your mother get to you."
Praising/Agreeing: "Well, *I* think you're a good worker."
Reassuring/Sympathizing: "You'll feel better tomorrow."
Denying/Diverting: "Don't worry about it. It's not that bad."
Me Too: "I know how you feel. Let me tell you what happened
     to me."

Analytic Stoppers trigger paralysis through analysis. When you analyze, lecture, or ask questions, you run the risk of eventually angering your partner. Besides not feeling understood, your spouse can feel patronized: "Don't you think I didn't think of that!"

### Analytic Stoppers

Teaching/Lecturing: "If you do thus and so, you won't have a
     problem."

Judging/Evaluating: "You're not being reasonable."
Interpreting/Analyzing: "It could be that time of the month again."
Probing/Questioning: "Why are you suddenly upset about this now?"

Aggressive Stoppers are the most harmful. That's when you criticize, bark orders, or belittle a partner to death: "It's ridiculous to feel that way and carry on like this," or "You're making a big thing out of nothing again." If your spouse wasn't angry at you before, he or she will be after you use these Stoppers.

### Aggressive Stoppers

Directing/Ordering: "Grow up and quit whining."
Warning/Threatening: "If you can't handle it, I'm leaving."
Criticizing/Blaming: "It's all your fault anyway. If you hadn't . . ."
Name Calling/Sarcasm: "You're being a big baby about it."
Moralizing/Shoulds: "You should stand up for yourself."

It's not engraved in stone that these are Stoppers all the time. But generally speaking, they tend to stop a partner from sharing. If you're tempted to use one of your stock Stoppers, listen constructively for a while before jumping in with your suggestions, lecture, or analysis.

Also, check in with your partner and ask what he or she would like: "Do you want some advice, or would you prefer that I just listen for a while?" That way you know exactly where you stand and how you can best lend support.

※

**Be aware of how you inadvertently stop your partner from sharing. By reducing Stoppers, you can decrease marital distance at midlife and begin to heal over past resentments.**

※

## Silence Is Indeed Golden

Think back to an argument you had with your spouse or perhaps an incident from childhood where you felt totally misunderstood. Remember how frustrating and painful that was? How alone you felt?

Well, the reverse is also true. Remember how comforting it was when someone listened in your hour of need and you felt heard? Perhaps it was one of your parents, a therapist, or a friend. The listener might not have said much, but you sensed that he or she understood. Suddenly, you were not alone nor crazy for feeling the way you did.

Because someone listened, you felt cared about as well. Remember that the next time your spouse is upset about something or has a problem. Simply by listening you give your partner the feeling that you care. Listening promotes intimacy. When your spouse shares something vulnerable and personal, and you're clear headed enough not to "stop" the process, your partner feels your presence and your support. For some couples, it can be more intimate than sex. Feeling listened to can be that important.

Being given the space to find one's own answer to a problem is also important, and being there with your partner is usually appreciated more than your advice, analysis, or other Stoppers. When you listen, get yourself out of the way so your partner has a chance to explore how he or she feels. It also shows that you have faith in your spouse to come to his or her own solution.

Silence, by the way, should not be confused with lack of involvement. We're not talking about half-listening while you quietly read the paper or attend to your own thoughts. The silence needed here is the silence of meditation combined with the concentration of a chess master. It's also much of what a therapist does for $100 an hour. The good news, according to both the research and our experience training couples, is that with a little practice, you can do it too.

❋

**Listen to your spouse with attentive silence when he or she shares a problem with you rather than jump in with quick advice or solutions. It's an excellent way to build intimacy.**

❋

### *Focus on Your Partner*

Once you've cleared your mind and stopped your Stoppers, focus on your partner. This nonverbal communication is a significant part of listening. One study on teachers concluded that nonverbal communication accounted for 80 percent of all interaction in the classroom. It's probably higher still in marriage, especially when emotions are stirred up.

Your eye contact is especially important. With good eye contact, your partner will feel closer to you, and connecting visually will further your concentration as well. If you have trouble making eye contact, don't expect to lock eyes like Don Juan. But don't cop out either. Add a little more eye contact each time you talk with your spouse. Practice on others, like the clerk at the cash register where you buy your groceries. If your partner has trouble with eye contact, don't overdo it. You don't want your spouse to feel pressured, invaded, or violated.

When your partner sends you an emotional message, think of it as an iceberg. The content of the communication is only the tip. Most of the message lies below the surface. The bulk of the iceberg is usually one of two things: a feeling your spouse is experiencing like anxiety, sadness, or anger, or an indirect statement or commentary about your relationship.

Take a common situation: Your partner says, "Chicken again," as you serve dinner. Depending on the tone of voice, there can be a lot of meat (pun intended) to the communication. If it's said with disappointment, that's the meat of the message, the bulk of the iceberg. The content, that chicken is being served again for dinner, is minor. The important news here is how your partner *feels* about the dinner.

Besides the feeling, there may be a relationship message here as well. Your partner may be asking you indirectly not to serve chicken again. That kind of message is tougher to hear and is frequently the bread and butter of marital conflict. Sometimes the relationship message is what we would like to say, but are afraid to.

Then again, depending on your partner's tone of voice, he or she could be happy about chicken being served again. Although the content or words of the message might still be "Chicken again," the meaning completely changes. It's important when you listen to hear the feeling or relationship message behind the words.

*You also might learn something when you listen, like I did in the example we shared earlier where Cathy accused me of making too many of her decisions for her. She was right. Telling her friend that Cathy couldn't work on the school bond issue because she needed to work on this book was definitely out of line. I was controlling her out of my own anxiety about writing the book! By listening, I was able to hear something I needed to hear.*

*Had I been defensive, even if only in my mind, I would not have heard that. It's the kind of issue that if left untended, could fester and become a huge boil later on. Take care of things early, and you prevent serious disease from threatening the life of this delicate psychological organism known as an ongoing, intimate relationship.*

❁

**The meat of a marital communication is either the feeling
your spouse has or the commentary he or she makes
about the relationship. Good listening can nip
these problems in the bud.**

❁

### *Let Your Partner Know You're Listening with Sliders*

Let's assume you've got your act together and you're listening attentively. If you're focusing on your partner and giving good eye contact, your spouse probably feels that you're fully present. But sometimes it helps to give them proof that you really are listening, especially if you have a quiet personality.

That's where Sliders come in. They up the activity level a bit on your side of the communication to let your partner know that you're listening. They also "slide" the conversation along in two important ways. First, Sliders make the listening process feel less one-sided or stilted. They also encourage your spouse to explore how he or she feels and to continue sharing.

Sliders, those little empathic grunts like "uh huh" or "hmm," let your spouse know you're following the conversation and are interested in what's being shared. Head nodding is also an effective Slider. It gives your partner visual evidence that you're listening. When we lecture at our seminars, it always amazes us how we tend to aim our presentation more at people in the audience who nod their heads in agreement. That movement by our listeners lets us know we're communicating our message.

Try it yourself the next time you're in a group of people. If you either nod your head or give a slight "uh huh," whoever is talking will likely talk more in your direction. It not only slides the conversation along, but it slides it your way as well. We're not suggesting you become like one of those bobbing heads that sometimes sits on the dash of a '55 Chevy. But it helps to up your activity level as a listener, especially if you tend to be passive and quiet.

More active Sliders are responses like "Wow" or "That's really interesting." Give yourself time to become comfortable with Sliders if they're new behaviors for you. Like any untrained course of action, they may feel foreign or artificial at first until you get used to them.

❋

**Let your partner know that you're listening by using Sliders, little empathic grunts like "uh huh" or nodding your head. Sliders encourage your spouse to share.**

❋

# Dynamic Listening

Once you've mastered the skills of stopping the Stoppers, focusing on your partner, and Sliders, you're ready to graduate to the most powerful technique, Dynamic Listening. Basically, it's a two-step process not unlike active listening, which has been used in other marital and parenting programs. First, you identify how your partner feels, the meat of the message. Then you feed it back. As with Sliders, it proves to your spouse that you've been listening. It's even more powerful, however, because you feed back to your spouse his or her exact feelings.

*Dynamic Listening bailed me out in that example where Cathy was upset with me for controlling too many of her decisions.*

Cathy: *"You've been telling me what to do now for the last several days! Last night Kate told me that you said I couldn't help her with the school bond issue because we had a book to write. You also decided I shouldn't bid on some items at the preschool auction. Well, you don't make my decisions!"*

*After overcoming my initial defensiveness, I realized that she was legitimately upset and needed to feel heard. So I employed the two steps of Dynamic Listening. I identified in my own mind how Cathy was feeling, and then I fed it back to her. Her chief feeling was anger.*

Steve: *"So basically you're angry at me because you feel like I'm making decisions about your life for you."*

*She immediately began to calm down, for she felt heard and understood on a deep level about a strongly felt issue. My tone of voice here was crucial, for had I sounded sarcastic or incredulous, the content of my feedback might have been accurate, but the meaning of the message would have been entirely different.*

*Rather than being ignored or negated, hearing her words and feelings affirmed and fed back to her gave Cathy the positive experience of feeling cared for, even of being loved. Whereas blocked feelings create distance, genuine listening builds intimacy. It's the single most effective tool you can use to renew your relationship at midlife, to tear down that wall between you and your partner that may have built up over the years.*

When you're upset and your spouse doesn't hear you, you can feel frustrated, misunderstood, thwarted, and unheard. There's no psychological connection between you and your partner. Chess master Boris Spassky once described himself and his first wife as being like bishops of a different color. Because the bishops move along the diagonal, they travel exclusively on either the white or black squares of the chess board. They never meet. Likewise, couples who don't listen effectively share the same game board, the same psychological space, but they never touch. There is no emotional connection.

And connection is what intimacy and relationships are all about. It's what gives our lives meaning. Whether we try to connect with God, Mother Nature, or our family and friends, it's often in that moment of connection that we feel validated, alive, important, and loved. We lose our sense of separateness, alienation, and aloneness.

It's crucial in the sexual relationship as well. Besides the physical release, which we can get through masturbation, connecting with someone beyond ourselves is what drives us to pursue sexual intimacy. For in that intimate dance of the sexual relationship, we are most keenly alive. Our very bodies tingle and vibrate from the touch of being known by our partner. Which is why the Bible refers to sex as "knowing" the other person, and why we feel "touched" by a shared intimacy.

The exciting news here is that you don't need a Ph.D. to be an effective listener. You can do this for your partner with a little practice, and in the process not only renew your relationship at midlife, but reach new heights of intimacy and personal growth as well.

Not only did Cathy feel heard in the above example, but when her anger was fed back to her, it cleared the field of a potentially deadly mine. For once it was listened to, it was disarmed. Cathy no longer needed to keep pressing the issue. Moreover, she didn't need to withdraw to lick her wounds in isolation. What was once a potentially explosive problem became a nonissue simply, and almost magically, by being genuinely and compassionately heard and understood.

Communication is at the root of a successful, intimate relationship. It is the means by which we share who we are with others, the bridge connecting us with our partners. It is the mingling of souls and the window through which we escape the prison of our individual loneliness. Good communication keeps the passageway clear, the field vibrant and open to new possibilities, and our marriages at midlife forever young.

### CHAPTER 6

# Getting Your Partner
# to Meet Your Needs

We cannot always oblige,
but we can always speak obligingly.
—Voltaire

Nancy and Barry were typical dual-career baby boomers. After twenty years together, they had two
teenagers, two sports utility vehicles, and too high a
mortgage. Like many working couples, they were also too busy
to maintain their relationship.

"I haven't felt close to Barry for several years now," Nancy
said during a family therapy session for their seventeen-year-
old son Toby. "Now that Jessica is gone and Toby's about to
leave home, I'm afraid Barry and I won't have much to keep
us together."

Nancy worked forty hours a week as a bookkeeper for a
large winery. She also helped her mom during the week with
her dad, who had Alzheimer's. Clearly, this was a woman who
was spread too thin.

But that was only half the problem. Although her marriage had been hectic when the kids were little, Nancy wasn't as angry at Barry then as she was now at midlife. She was tired of his lack of initiative as a provider, and his increasingly biting wit had driven her away emotionally. The distance between them had grown wider over the years.

When we asked Nancy if she had spoken to Barry about her concerns, she answered that she was afraid to: "He'd probably say something sarcastic, and I'd only get hurt again. Besides," she continued, "he should know why I've pulled away by now."

Barry felt Nancy's resentment as well as her distance, but he *didn't* know why. For his part, he was hurt by her disdain. We asked him the same question we asked her: Had he shared his concerns? Did he let her know that he needed to feel accepted and loved? He replied, "Well, sort of, but isn't it obvious?"

Evidently it wasn't, which is not surprising. The problem here is that each had succumbed to the communication myth "If you loved me, you'd know how I feel." As with many couples at midlife, they also believed in a variant of that myth: "If you loved me, you'd know how I've changed." This too, as we shall see, can seriously jeopardize a relationship during the middle years.

❋

**One of the biggest challenges to an ongoing relationship at midlife is having the courage to risk sharing how you feel and how your needs may have changed over the years.**

❋

## The Courage to Be
## Who You've Become

Freud thought that dreams expressed unconscious wishes. Others believe they provide answers. Nancy's dream did both. It fulfilled her desire for intimacy while providing a blueprint, literally, for how to restructure her marriage.

In it she walked through a house with a hard hat on her head and construction plans under her arm. It was her home, but the rooms had all changed. The wall between the living room and the den had been torn down, and a skylight and large deck had been added to the bedroom. She felt confused, but confident. By the time she lay back to sun herself on her new deck, she was smiling.

Then she woke up. Her bedroom was as dark as ever and there was still a wall separating the den from the rest of the house. Her dream, she later realized, represented the change she was going through at midlife. Her new home was symbolic of the new relationship she now desired with her husband.

"I often read in the living room while Barry watches TV in the den," she reflected. "It feels like we're miles apart. In the dream, it felt great not to have that wall between us! And the bedroom," she continued, "always feels dark and gloomy, just like our sex life. That's why the new skylight and deck felt like such a breath of fresh air."

In her dream, Nancy had restructured her life. It was now time to do it for real, but how?

## *Take Responsibility for How You Feel*

It may sound like so much California psychobabble, but taking responsibility for how you feel is crucial if you're to restructure your relationship at midlife. It's the first step in finding the courage to be who you've become. It means, among other things, that how you feel is ultimately your doing, not your partner's. He or she may have done something to cause you pain, but it's still your hurt, your loneliness, and your pain. It's up to *you* to deal with it.

In Nancy's case, it meant taking action. Complaining week after week in therapy about "Barry this" and "Barry that" might provide some relief for a day or two, but it wouldn't change anything at home. Nancy first had to realize *her* role in the problem. Only then could she do something about it.

As is common with relationship problems, theirs was an escalating cycle. Like a law of physics, each partner's action fueled an equal but opposite reaction by the other spouse. For example, the more sarcastic Barry became, the more Nancy withdrew. The more she withdrew, the more abandoned Barry felt, and the more likely he was to lash out in anger, thus repeating the cycle.

One way to break that cycle was for each partner to do his or her part. Nancy, for instance, couldn't work on whether Barry was sarcastic or not. She had no control there. She *did* have control, however, on her half of the equation: whether to withdraw or not. By altering her part in the cycle, she could change it.

Which is one good reason why you should take responsibility for your role in a relationship problem. You become less of a passive victim and more of an empowered player. In Nancy's case, it would be like putting on the hard hat and knocking down a few walls. By taking "response-ability" for her half of the problem, Nancy increased her ability to respond.

❋

**Take "response-ability" for your part of a marital problem.**
**It increases your ability to respond and empowers**
**you  with more control to restructure your**
**relationship at midlife.**

❋

### "If You Loved Me, You'd Know How I've Changed"

Carl Sandburg wrote that "nothing happens unless first a dream." Nancy had the dream. Now she needed to make it happen.

Midlife change often begins with a similar daydream, fantasy, or wish. After years of gradual maturation (a word whose Latin root means "to ripen"), suddenly the fruit falls from the tree. What appears as a sudden change at midlife often begins as a dream years earlier.

Midlife couples often harbor the mistaken belief that each spouse will somehow know how the other has changed and recognize what the other now needs. Don't hold your breath.

People rarely know how you feel unless you tell them. This includes your partner.

One of the reasons this is such a tempting myth is that sometimes your partner *does* know. Studies show that spouses learn to recognize one another's nonverbal behavior, for instance. But that doesn't mean your partner knows all the time, or even half the time. And even when your spouse identifies that you're troubled or agitated, frequently he or she doesn't know why. That's especially likely if you haven't spoken much over the years, which is not uncommon for many couples at midlife.

Barry, for instance, sensed Nancy's distance and withdrawal, but he had no idea it was because of his sarcastic wit. In fact, he thought it was due to menopause. Nancy, for her part, didn't realize that much of Barry's sarcasm stemmed from his anger because he felt unloved by her.

For this couple to rekindle their relationship, they couldn't assume that the other spouse knew how they felt or why.

※

**Don't buy the communication myth "If you loved me, you'd know how I've changed." Your partner probably won't know how your needs have changed at midlife until you voice them.**

※

### Be Congruent: Tell It Like It Is

Assuming you're ready to voice your needs, how do you do it effectively? Well, consider becoming "congruent," a model developed by renowned psychologist Carl Rogers.[1]

We trained at and helped staff one of his programs in the early 1970s. His ideas on congruence greatly influenced us when we later developed our first marital communications class back in 1975.

Basically, there are three levels of congruence (see diagram below). First, you're someone who has needs and feelings, however you may not be aware of them. For example, when you're upset about something, but can't quite put your finger on what's bothering you. Your emotions aren't in congruence with your awareness; they don't match. Essentially, you're out of touch with your feelings.

For instance, when Barry is shut out by Nancy, he feels hurt and rejected, but he's not aware of how he feels. It's one of the reasons he indirectly attacks her with angry sarcasm. In fact, when Nancy defends herself by saying, "Well, you don't have to get so angry," Barry responds, with anger in his voice, "I'm not angry!" He means it too, because his awareness is not in congruence with how he feels.

## CONGRUENCE

STAGE ONE
Needs & Feelings
*(Below Consciousness)*

STAGE TWO
Awareness
*(Conscious Thought)*

STAGE THREE
Behavior
*(Social Action)*

The second stage of congruence is when you get in touch with how you feel. You become aware of your feelings. Rather than sulk about the house under some vague veil of depression, for example, your self-talk becomes more enlightened: "We never go anywhere together anymore. I miss that!" You become conscious of what was previously unconscious. Your thoughts are in congruence with your feelings; you know what bothers you.

Barry reached the second stage of congruence when he became aware of feeling hurt and rejected by Nancy. Rather than being out of touch with his sarcastic tone of voice, he now recognized how shut out he felt at this stage of midlife. His awareness was now in congruence with how he felt about his marriage. Note, however, that he still hasn't talked to Nancy about it yet.

That's stage three: when you *act* in congruence with your awareness and your feelings. Basically, you put it all together. At stage two, you became aware internally of how you felt, but you haven't *done* anything about it yet. At stage three, not only are you aware that you feel lonely and detached in your relationship, for example, but you take action in congruence with your awareness and your feelings. You talk to your partner about it.

Which is ultimately what Barry needs to do. He must first become aware of how he feels and then share what he discovers about himself with his wife, Nancy. He needs to interact socially in congruence with his thoughts and feelings.

This is no easy task, for it will take considerable courage to risk sharing his vulnerability. The bottom line, however, is that in order to renew his relationship at midlife, he'll need to muster the courage to tell it like it is, to reveal what he feels and who he's become.

❉

**To get your needs met at midlife, be congruent. Become aware of how your needs and feelings may have changed. Then have the courage to risk sharing them with your partner.**

❉

### Be Assertive: Attack the Problem, Not Your Partner

Do you feel neglected or lonely in your midlife relationship because your partner has changed and gone off in a new direction? How about trapped or controlled? It's often difficult to know whether to say anything, isn't it? Or if you do, exactly what to say.

No doubt you remember times when you said something, but wished you hadn't. You also probably can recall instances where you said nothing, but then felt resentful and distant.

Well, if you're looking to strike a middle position, consider becoming assertive. It's a technique we adapted from the book that pioneered the assertiveness movement, *Your Perfect Right*, written by psychologists Bob Alberti and Michael Emmons.[2]

Basically, it looks like this:

**PASSIVE                    ASSERTIVE                    AGGRESSIVE**

On the one extreme, you have being passive. That's when you feel hurt, angry, or any number of emotions, but you don't say anything. You stew on it. You feel lonely and disconnected from your partner, for instance, but you bottle it up inside.

As we've discussed, such blocked feelings likely create further distance as well as resentment. They are one of the greatest threats to your relationship at midlife, for it is often at that time that you reap the consequences of earlier years when you didn't share your gradually changing needs and feelings.

Don't confuse being passive and not saying anything, however, with counting to ten to rethink how you talk to yourself about your relationship. As we explored in part 2, dropping unrealistic expectations and challenging faulty assumptions can help reduce marital resentment and increase your relationship satisfaction.

If doing that doesn't change how you feel, however, don't continue to sit on issues. For then you're only being passive, not productive, and that can prove hazardous to marital health.

The other extreme is aggressive. That's when you tell your partner how you feel, but you attack your mate personally as you do it. Aggressive communication damages your spouse's self-esteem as well as your relationship.

If you feel abandoned when your partner plays golf or visits family, for instance, labeling him or her inconsiderate or selfish doesn't do much to solve the problem. Your spouse is likely to become defensive and either attack back or withdraw in quiet resentment. By blaming or attacking, you drive your mate further away, rather than bring him or her closer to you, which was the original goal of your communication.

Better to attack the problem, not your partner, by being assertive. This middle position avoids the pitfalls that come with the extremes of being passive or aggressive. You want to get your position out on the table, but in a way that your spouse will be able to hear it.

❋

**Don't be passive sharing your changing needs and
feelings, lest you build up resentment and distance.
Avoid being aggressive too, so you don't drive
your partner away. Best to be assertive.**

❋

## Assertive Sending

Imagine for a moment that you return home after playing extra sets in an extended championship tennis match. You're exhausted but exhilarated after winning your club's annual tournament. You look forward to showing your partner your new trophy, but instead you're greeted with, "You've been gone all day. How can you always be so selfish and inconsiderate?!"

Feeling empathetic? Probably not. You're likely either to head for the door or fire back an angry retort. And who could blame you (other than your spouse, of course)? Why? Because you feel criticized and verbally assaulted.

If your spouse was feeling neglected or lonely at this stage in your midlife relationship, you might have a hard time deciphering that, especially in the heat of the moment when you're under attack. Your mate wasn't being congruent or assertive, so the message wasn't sent in a clear or straightforward manner.

But it can be. Had your spouse tried what we call Assertive Sending, you might have been more receptive.

## I *vs.* You *Statements*

A key part of Assertive Sending is the use of *I* rather than *you* statements. A crucial problem in the above example, for instance, is that your spouse focused exclusively on *you*, rather than sharing how he or she felt. Such *you* statements are at the root of much marital conflict and dissolution. They're similar to what psychologist Tom Gordon calls "you-messages" in his excellent book *Parent Effectiveness Training*.[3] They're as harmful and ineffective maritally as they are in parenting.

Notice your partner's choice of words: *"You've* been gone all day. How can *you* always be so selfish and inconsiderate." That second *you* statement is especially harmful for two reasons. First, the word "always." As they say, never use the word "never" and always avoid "always." They're usually inaccurate and frequently trigger debate.

The second problem is name-calling, a major mistake in marital communication. Whether you're selfish or inconsiderate is speculation, not fact. You can probably ask three psychologists and get four opinions. At any rate, it will likely be disputed, especially by you.

How about if your partner said this instead: "I've felt down all day. I guess I just missed you." Would you feel less defensive? Probably so. Why? Because you're not being attacked, for one thing. There's also no name-calling.

The key here is the shift from "you" to "I." Instead of blaming and criticizing you, your spouse shares how he or she feels.

Whereas you'll probably debate whether you're "selfish" or "inconsiderate," you're far less likely to dispute whether your partner felt "down" or "missed you." One is opinion; the other is fact.

❄

**Rather than attack your partner with "you statements,"**
**better to share your feelings with "I statements."**
**Change "You're inconsiderate and never around"**
**to "I miss you," for example.**

❄

### Watch Your Tone and Body Language

Using the right words is only half the battle, however. Your tone of voice and body language are also crucial.

Remember the example from the previous chapter where "Chicken again" was said as dinner was served? Those same two words can mean a variety of things depending upon your tone of voice. If you were disappointed, for instance, your tone would convey an entirely different message than if you were happy or surprised about again having chicken for dinner.

Even if you didn't say a word, your body language could speak volumes by itself. If you were disappointed, you might fold your arms across your chest, let out a long, slow sigh, and gaze dejectedly down at the table. If you loved this particular recipe for chicken, on the other hand, and were genuinely excited about eating it again, you might smile broadly, rub your hands together in anticipation, and look expectantly at the platter as it was passed around the table.

It's been said that when you put two people together, they cannot *not* communicate. Keep that in mind, especially when you're angry. Even if you're not openly or verbally aggressive, your tone still can be subtly sarcastic, condescending, or critical. Such passive-aggressive digs are like a steel hammer cloaked in a velvet glove; the damage to your relationship can be just as devastating.

❋

**Beware of your tone and body language, especially when you're angry. They can bite worse than the bark of your words.**

❋

### Ask Directly for What You Need

Another form of Assertive Sending is to ask for what you need. What is it that you need right now, for instance, in your midlife relationship? Do you need more independence? Intimacy? Whatever it is, avoid the extremes of being passive or aggressive and put "I need" or "I'd like" in front of what's missing for you currently.

But be specific, rather than global. "I'd like to spend some time with you" is a good start. However, it still might overwhelm or confuse your partner. Better to add a second sentence immediately after: "How about we go to the movies and then out to dinner this Saturday?"

Be realistic and ask for something concrete that meets your needs but doesn't threaten your partner. Often little changes go a long way. Your emotional climate is like a kaleidoscope: one small turn, and the whole picture shifts.

Remember, however, that even if you use your best Assertive Sending, your partner still has the right to say no. You're not entitled to get what you want just because you request it.

❀

**Ask directly for what you need. Be specific, concrete, and realistic. Like a kaleidoscope, one small change can dramatically transform how you feel about your marriage at midlife.**

❀

## *Make Deposits in Your Partner's Emotional Bank Account*

Even when you ask nicely, you still place a demand on your spouse for something. It's like making a withdrawal from your partner's emotional bank account. Too many requests over the years, and you break the bank. To avoid depleting your spouse's good will, make regular deposits so you have a cushion to draw from.

One way to do that is to share positives with your partner. They can be about the little things you appreciate day to day. The key is to become aware of those daily positive thoughts and feelings as they flicker across your consciousness, and then mention them to your mate.

For instance, when you open your drawer and see that your

partner has washed your favorite shirt, you might think to yourself for a brief moment "Oh great, my blue shirt!" Why not share that with your spouse? A simple "Thanks, babe, for doing the laundry" can boost your partner's morale, encourage your mate to continue doing the wash, improve how he or she feels about you and your relationship, and provide a reservoir of goodwill that you can draw on later when you need something down the line.

Not surprisingly, studies show that similar positive reinforcement by supervisors is as important to many workers as their paychecks. It's an inherent human need to feel appreciated by those around us. So consider sharing four positives with your partner for every negative. It will give you something to draw on during those difficult times of transition.

❋

**Give your spouse four positives for every negative.**
**By depositing positives into your partner's emotional**
**bank account, you don't dip into the red when**
**you need to make a withdrawal.**

❋

## Get Below Your Anger

This is essential to effectively renegotiate your relationship during midlife and a key factor in effective Assertive Sending. Anger is often a secondary reaction to a more primary emotion, such as loneliness or anxiety. When you lead with anger rather than your more vulnerable feelings underneath, you're more likely to threaten your partner and drive him or her further away.

For example, how would you *first* feel if your partner suddenly decided to change careers at midlife to one likely to earn considerably less income? If you weren't well off financially, you'd probably feel anxious and insecure. "How are we going to get the kids through college?" you might worry to yourself. "When will we ever get to retire?"

Immediately following on the heels of your anxiety, however, would also likely be anger. "How could you do this to us now?!" you might fume. "I thought we had an agreement!" You could voice your anger, but your more primary emotion is anxiety. You're angry *because* you feel vulnerable, threatened, and betrayed.

Which feeling you share with your partner will seriously impact how effective you are at negotiating this bend in your marital journey. As you know from firsthand experience, anger is the tougher emotion to handle. It increases the likelihood that your spouse will get defensive.

If you lead with the softer, more primary feeling of anxiety, it's no guarantee that your partner will listen to you, but it ups the odds that he or she will. Your mate's more likely to drop his or her defensive posture and open up to your concerns. The bottom line is that if you want to be understood, you need to talk in a way that your partner will be able to hear.

&#42;

**Anger is usually a secondary reaction to a more primary emotion, such as anxiety or loneliness. Get below your anger. Your spouse will be more likely to hear you.**

&#42;

*For example, Steve told a therapist colleague of mine, Linda, who is also a writer, how "he" wrote the proposal for this book and how "he" got our agent. During the entire ten-minute phone conversation, he didn't use the word "we" once!*

*I was angry, but I took some of our own advice and reflected for a few minutes on my "self-talk" before talking with my partner. It didn't take long to realize that I felt hurt about being left out, a common button for me being the youngest of three siblings.*

*Once I became more congruent within myself, I decided to try some Assertive Sending with Steve: "I felt hurt and left out when you kept saying 'I' instead of 'we' when you talked about our book with Linda." Steve felt badly and apologized for hurting my feelings.*

*Had I accused him of being narcissistic and self-centered, for instance (something we both acknowledge is his area of weakness), he would have become, justifiably, defensive. It helped that I didn't send such* you *statements. It also was essential that I got below my anger.*

### Write Your Spouse a Letter

Another way to communicate your needs and feelings at midlife is to write rather than speak to your partner, although talking things over after exchanging letters is a nice combination.

One of the benefits of writing is that it helps you collect your thoughts. Even if you never give your spouse the letter, you become more aware of what troubles you. Writing also serves as an emotional release valve. Some people let go of most of their immediate relationship frustration just by writing down how they feel about it.

Another key advantage is that you don't get interrupted. When you talk to your spouse about a heated relationship issue, you can only expect your partner to listen for two or three minutes at a time. Typically, your mate then expects equal time and needs you to listen to him or her for a while in return. By writing, you can explain how you feel in greater detail.

You also have time to choose your words more carefully, which is in your spouse's best interest as well as your own. This is especially valuable when you're angry, for as the Roman philosopher Seneca once wrote, "The greatest remedy for anger is delay."

Finally, your partner has time to read between the lines and to digest your words, thus ensuring that your position gets understood more thoroughly. It also gives your spouse more control over the process, which is to your advantage. When a marital partner feels overwhelmed in conversation, he or she is more apt to get defensive and less likely to listen.

Keep it short and edit your work. Your spouse will be more inclined to read two well-organized pages rather than five rambling ones. Also, incorporate your best Assertive Sending techniques: don't attack, get below your anger, suggest simple, concrete solutions, and sprinkle a liberal dose of positives throughout. It's okay to ask your partner to write back, but ask nicely, and give your mate a few days to respond.

*

**Writing helps you collect your thoughts, pick your words more carefully, and share your position without being interrupted. However, keep it short, avoid attacks, and be positive.**

*

### Take Assertive Action

All communication need not be verbal or implied. Action is a powerful language as well. Consider taking assertive action to get what you need.

*Let me give you an example. Steve woke up and did his usual exercise routine. I was about to head off to work, but I missed feeling connected with him and wanted a hug before I left.*

*So I cuddled up to him on the floor while he exercised, and we hugged for a moment there. I got my needs met, and because I was positive (and brief), Steve didn't feel like I violated his space.*

*In order to pull this off, however, I first had to avoid two common forms of negative relationship self-talk. First, I didn't set myself up with the faulty assumption that "He should know that I need a hug before I go." Such a passive posture could build resentment and trigger distance or an aggressive attack later down the line.*

*I also could have sparked some trouble with this equally common, faulty assumption: "It's not a fulfilling hug unless Steve initiates it." While it would be preferable if your partner initiates a desired behavior, it should not be mandatory.*

✻

**Take assertive action to meet your relationship needs. For instance, initiate a hug or cuddle with your partner, rather than blame your spouse because you feel distant.**

✻

Odds are good that what you need from your relationship may change significantly during your middle years. How well you communicate with your partner about your changing desires will dramatically affect your marital satisfaction. Learn to talk about your needs for independence, intimacy, security, and support, for instance, in ways that your spouse will be able to hear.

It's especially important to have the courage to risk sharing who you are as well as your hopes and fears for the future. Through Assertive Sending, you can avoid much of the frustration and isolation that plagues many couples in ongoing intimate relationships. It is a key to rekindling your marriage at midlife.

### CHAPTER 7

# Win-Win Relationships

Don't find fault. Find a remedy.

—Henry Ford

et's assume that you get below your anger and become a model of Assertive Sending, but your spouse still responds with opposition and resistance. Now what?

Well, that happened to us recently, and on Valentine's Day no less. Instead of cupid shooting sweet little arrows through our hearts, we two marriage experts fired shots across each other's bow.

*Cathy went for a walk with her friends rather than edit a chapter I had just finished. She felt pressured and controlled. I felt unimportant and abandoned.*

*So I practiced what I preach. First, I wrote in my journal to clarify what I was feeling, which did help some, especially to get below my anger. I realized how I now looked forward to being with my wife more than I did during our earlier years. Moreover, some of what I was feeling were old issues from childhood being tripped off by our current marital transition.*

Cathy was doing more things separately than ever before. Also in the last year, our oldest son left home to go to college, and the youngest one disappeared soon after he got his driver's license. As Cathy said mid-argument: "I enjoy the freedom of the kids being gone and not placing everyone's needs above my own. It's my turn now."

I felt cast aside, an emotion that stirred up old memories of when my younger brother was born and I was moved upstairs to sleep in the attic. The marital transition was a one-alarm blaze, but I reacted as if it were a four-alarm fire. Only in this case, I wasn't being replaced by my younger brother, but by Cathy's friends.

Making these connections helped calm me down. My self-talk became more realistic as well. But I still needed to share with Cathy how I needed to feel more important to her, so I tried some Assertive Sending.

"Sorry I was upset earlier when I wanted you to edit that chapter," I began. "I know I'm overreacting, but I need to feel more important in your list of priorities, and I felt cast aside when you went for that walk with Connie, Marcia, and Kathy."

It wasn't a bad message. I didn't attack in anger, shared my vulnerability, and even acknowledged my responsibility for overreacting. But as we often say to couples, just because you voice it well doesn't mean that your spouse won't have a reaction of his or her own. In this case, Cathy did.

"I don't like it when you try to control my schedule," she responded. "I'm willing to edit that chapter, but I shouldn't have to drop everything just because it's convenient for you. What about my plans? I've got friends waiting that I really enjoy being with."

Then she added something that was difficult to hear, yet an

*honest reflection of a classic midlife transition. "I love you, but I need other things as well, especially my friends."*

*This was somewhat new in our relationship. We had always prioritized either the marriage or the family, however now Cathy was reshuffling the deck, and a wild card was beginning to surface: her desire for more separateness. As we talked about in chapter 3, this is not unusual for many women during their middle years.*

What began with Assertive Sending for one spouse became a classic midlife, relationship conflict. Remember: Just because *your* needs change at midlife doesn't mean your partner is going to like it or that his or her needs haven't changed as well.

To negotiate win-win solutions that satisfy your mate as well as yourself, you'll need to use both the listening and the assertion skills we talked about in the previous two chapters. But you'll need to use them both at the same time.

❋

**Even when you effectively share your changing relationship needs at midlife, your spouse won't necessarily meet them. Be prepared for conflict as your partner may have changed as well.**

❋

## Renegotiate Your Relationship

Remember how when you move one part of a mobile, the entire structure changes? Well, the same is often true when relationships change at midlife, for when one of you shifts direction, the other one typically needs to correct course too.

So how can you do this effectively? By using a three-step negotiating process called the ABCs of Harmonizing. Besides guiding you and your partner as you rationally address the issues between you, Harmonizing helps you brainstorm alternatives as well as choose or contract a solution.

## THE ABCs OF HARMONIZING

A: Address Midlife Change
B: Brainstorm Alternatives
C: Choose or Contract a Solution

### A: Address Midlife Change

The A in these ABCs of Harmonizing is for addressing both your positions in a way that respects your needs and feelings as well as your spouse's.

You can't get to rational problem solving until you bleed the emotional noise out of the system. That's where listening comes in, and why it's so important; it's the bread and butter of conflict resolution. You won't get to first base until each of you feels heard and your opinions valued.

Neither of which is likely if you or your partner feels criticized or attacked. This is why Assertive Sending is also crucial during this phase of Harmonizing. Because emotions run high during this sensitive stage, a few aggressive *you* statements can derail the entire process.

Not only is it important to lower the emotional pressure,

it's also essential to understand what your partner needs from you at this juncture in your relationship. You can't satisfy your spouse until you know what he or she needs, nor can you be satisfied without your spouse's knowing what you need. Any agreement that doesn't fulfill both of you will likely be sabotaged by the dissatisfied partner. You both must address the midlife change in your relationship.

❋

**The A in the ABCs of Harmonizing is for addressing your changing marital needs at midlife. Listening is crucial. If either of you don't feel heard, negotiations go nowhere.**

❋

There are three formats you can use to address your midlife stalemate. Each provides different guidelines to help structure your negotiation and keep you on task. The Emotional Barometer and the Letter Exchange you can do without your partner's having to read the book, although it's considerably easier if your spouse reads the three communication chapters in this section and is up to speed on what you're trying to do. Because the Give and Take is a more sophisticated technique, your spouse must read these chapters before he or she will be able to participate.

## USE THE EMOTIONAL BAROMETER
## TO LOWER PARTNER'S "PRESSURE"

Let's be realistic. For example, when you tell your partner that you need more intimacy at this stage in your midlife relationship, your partner may get defensive and take the opposite tack. "Well, I'm sorry," he or she might say, if you're lucky enough to get such a polite response, "but I really enjoy my work."

Now what? Well, try the Emotional Barometer. If your spouse feels pressured by your needs, for instance, listen down that emotional pressure or defensiveness with either Dynamic Listening or one of the other listening techniques. Remember: You won't get very far with *your* needs if your spouse doesn't feel heard on his or hers.

Essentially, you need to do three things. First, craft and rehearse your basic position. Keep it simple, stick to the issue, and boil it down to one sentence, if possible. Then use your best Assertive Sending to get below your anger and ask for what you need.

Second, when your spouse reacts defensively, listen down his or her emotional pressure. Remember: Even if you voice your position well, you're still putting pressure on your partner. Be sensitive, and listen to your spouse's reaction. Dynamic Listening will prove especially effective at this point. You want your mate to feel heard, so that when you send your message again, he or she will be more willing to listen.

Which is basically step three: sharing your message again after listening down your partner's defensiveness. Keep your communication simple at this point too. Because you listened down your partner's emotional pressure, you're now more likely to get heard on the second go-around.

All this is easier said than done, however (even for us, and we teach this stuff). It's tempting to deceive yourself with the illusion that because your position makes such elegant sense to *you*, it will to your partner as soon as your mate hears the "wisdom" of your position. Don't believe it. Remind yourself that your spouse will likely see things from an entirely different point of view. So prepare yourself to listen, even before you open your mouth.

*This is what I did in my conversation with Cathy. After taking a few minutes to choose my words carefully, I psyched myself up to listen to whatever I got back in response. I also watched my timing. "Got a moment?" I asked, even before beginning my Assertive Sending.*

*When Cathy gave me the green light, I then delivered the message I shared with you at the beginning of this chapter, which is also step one of the Emotional Barometer: "Sorry I was upset earlier when I wanted you to edit that chapter. I know I'm overreacting, but I need to feel more important in your list of priorities, and I felt cast aside when you went for that walk with Connie, Marcia, and Kathy."*

*As you know, she didn't respond with "My poor sweet baby." She fired back instead: "I don't like it when you try to control my schedule. I'm willing to edit that chapter, but I shouldn't have to drop everything just because it's convenient for you. What about my plans? I've got friends waiting that I really enjoy being with." Adding insult to injury, she added, "I love you, but I need other things as well, especially my friends."*

*This is a critical juncture where many midlife negotiations break down. Think about all the tempting rebuttals I could make at this point, like, "Who's more important, your friends or your husband?"*

*We could rapidly escalate to uproar over her friends vs. me, each attacking, with nobody listening. Or Cathy could knuckle under out of guilt, but underneath she'd resent me for stunting her autonomy and ignoring her need for separateness at this stage in her life. Either way, the relationship would lose.*

*Which is why it's crucial to acknowledge your spouse's point of view, to bring it out on the table along with your own. Yours isn't the only fine wine that needs to breathe. With that in mind, I went to step two of the Emotional Barometer. I listened down her position, using Dynamic Listening: "It sounds like you feel controlled by me, and that gets pretty irritating, especially when you've already made plans. It also sounds like your friends are becoming increasingly important to you."*

*The key here is that Cathy's reaction is acknowledged rather than dismissed, even though it's 180 degrees different from mine. By feeding her feelings back to her, we lower her emotional pressure. She is less likely then to get defensive or to withdraw in angry silence.*

*She also becomes more receptive to hearing my basic position the second time around, the final step of the Emotional Barometer. "I'm sorry, babe," I continued, repeating the gist of my original message. "I didn't mean to pressure you. I guess I just felt cast aside and unimportant."*

*Now notice what happens. She hears me, even apologizes for hurting my feelings, and offers to make it up to me by spending the afternoon together! "I'm sorry," she responded. "I didn't mean to abandon you. How about after I edit that chapter, we do something fun?"*

*Like the Biblical principle "As ye sow, so shall ye reap," attacking begets more attacking, whereas giving and listening reap a more positive harvest of love and understanding. We hugged, and the encounter was over, all in the course of five minutes. Think how long an unresolved conflict with its ensuing distance could have lasted!*

The Emotional Barometer is a great technique to use whenever your partner's pressure rises. The key here is to use

Dynamic Listening to listen down that pressure or defensiveness so that your partner is able to hear you the second, or third time around.

Don't be surprised, by the way, if it takes several go-arounds. As long as you're prepared to listen, you stand an excellent chance of getting heard yourself.

❋

**Be realistic. When you share your changing needs at midlife, your partner may react defensively. By listening down your spouse's emotional pressure, you're more likely to get heard.**

❋

## TO AVOID BEING INTERRUPTED, USE THE LETTER EXCHANGE

If all this sounds too difficult, try the Letter Exchange. It's easier to articulate your position when you don't have to contend with your spouse's reactions. As we outlined in chapter 6, writing helps you collect your thoughts, pick your words more carefully, and share your position without being interrupted.

All of which are especially helpful when you try to address such a complex and sensitive subject as how your marital needs may have changed at midlife. This is not something that can be easily explained in a sound bite.

Ask your mate to respond to your letter, but give your spouse the option of either talking to you about the issues you raised or writing back, depending on what's comfortable for your partner. After several days, if you haven't heard anything, ask. But watch your timing. Long car rides or over dinner at a restaurant are generally good.

＊

**Use the Letter Exchange if combining listening and**
**sending feels too overwhelming. Writing lets you develop**
**your position without being interrupted by**
**your partner's defensive reactions.**

＊

## GIVE AND TAKE TO ADDRESS CHANGING NEEDS

Another effective way you can address your midlife stalemate is to use what we call the Give and Take, but you'll need your spouse to read the three communication chapters in this section of the book. Basically with this format, you take turns listening.

Your partner talks for a minute or two while you listen, then you reverse roles, and you talk while your partner listens. To ensure that you're hearing one another, it helps if each of you feeds back the gist of your mate's position before taking a turn yourselves. But you can also agree to just silently listen instead.

We suggest you use an egg timer or one of those hour glasses from a board game that only goes for a minute or two. It's important that you stop when your time is up, otherwise the boundaries of whose turn it is become blurred, and conflict can develop. It's especially important to stop talking if you're the more vocal spouse.

When it's your floor, remember to avoid name-calling, criticism, and other forms of aggressive communication. Use your best Assertive Sending. Remember: You want your partner to hear you, not turn you off. You're free to respond to your partner's previous statements or take the ball in another direction.

Generally, however, it's good to stick to one subject at a time and respond to the issues raised by your spouse.

Keep a spirit of inquiry. You don't want to defeat your partner. Ultimately, a win-win solution depends on both your positions being heard and understood. With that in mind, seek to learn as much as you can about how your spouse feels, what your partner needs at this phase of your relationship, and why your mate feels the way he or she does.

Also, don't misinterpret your spouse's needs as a challenge to your autonomy or security. Look at your partner and listen as if he or she were a friend, not your mate. You'll be less likely then to take what your spouse says as a personal threat or affront.

The Give and Take is an excellent format to use when you find yourselves in the midst of an argument. Say something like, "Look, we're not hearing one another. Why don't we try that Give and Take? I'll listen first." That last sentence is important, for your spouse will be more likely to play ball when he or she gets to bat first.

If emotions run too high, agree ahead of time that either of you can ask for a time-out. Whoever does, however, should set a specific time to reconvene so the other partner isn't left hanging. Remember not to attack as you exit. The following *I* statement is a good example of how to ask for a cease-fire: "I'm overwhelmed right now and don't think I can continue. Let's take a break and pick this up again after lunch."

※

**The Give and Take is an excellent format to plug into when you're arguing. It ensures that each of you gets heard. Use an egg or game timer to signal whose turn it is to talk.**

※

## B: Brainstorm Alternatives

Once you've addressed your differences successfully, you're ready for the B in the ABCs of Harmonizing: Brainstorming. Here you generate possible solutions to your midlife stalemate. A word of warning, however: You won't pass "Go" if either of you doesn't feel heard. Brainstorming assumes that you're able to be reasonable. You won't be if you're still angry at your partner for not understanding or valuing what you need at this stage in your relationship.

Assuming that you've cleared the emotional noise out of your marital system and that both of you understand each other's needs, it's time to find a solution to your midlife dilemma. Rather than haggle over one or two alternatives, better to generate more options. The more choices you have, the more likely you are to find one you both like. It's important at this stage to be creative.

For your edification and amusement, consider the following brainteaser: Try to connect the nine dots below with four straight lines without lifting your pencil off the paper.

.  .  .

.  .  .

.  .  .

Give up? Well, odds are you stayed within your preconceived boundary of the problem. If you do, you can't solve it.

The solution exists only when you expand your perceptual set. (Turn to page 172 to check out the answer.)

This nine-dot problem is like many marital dilemmas at midlife; when you limit your options to begin with, it's harder to find a creative solution. Often the answer lies beyond the three or four choices you and your partner allowed yourselves to consider. So rather than get into a battle for control over one or two options, look beyond your usual perceptual boundaries to discover a range of solutions you hadn't considered before. For when it comes to brainstorming, rule number one is to get creative.

Rule number two is to list every possibility, no matter how zany. This isn't the time to choose "the" solution. That comes later when you get to the C in the ABCs of Harmonizing, choosing or contracting. For now, you want to free up your creative juices.

You also don't want to anger your spouse by dismissing one of his or her pet ideas. And don't editorialize by raising your eyebrows or smirking at suggestions. Remember that your tone of voice and body language can communicate more than your words. For the moment, allow everything. You'll get a chance to veto any and all options during the C phase.

Generally speaking, it's best to list at least eight possible solutions. Also, take turns brainstorming so you and your partner don't feel dominated by one another. As you can see, this is not a process you can do in five minutes. Allow at least half an hour for each stage of Harmonizing.

*It took Cathy and me about an hour to Harmonize our plans for a recent vacation to Hawaii. It was time well spent.*

*Haggling over money has ruined many a family vacation in the past. Pressuring the kids to order cheap meals is not my wife's idea of fun in the sun.*

*After hearing one another using the Give and Take, we brainstormed several options. It was challenging for me not to roll my eyes when Cathy suggested that I just "go with the flow" and not look at the Visa bill the following month. And I'm sure it wasn't easy for her when I suggested that the kids pay their own way when we ate out so they could learn the value of a dollar. But we listed all our options, including several more moderate ones.*

*But before we tell you what we settled on, here's the answer to that nine-dot problem:*

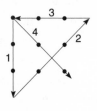

✸

**The B in the ABCs of Harmonizing is for brainstorming alternatives to your midlife dilemma. Be creative and list everything.**

✸

## C: Choose or Contract a Solution

Here you get to choose one or combine several of the options you brainstormed to form a new midlife contract with your partner. In this final stage of Harmonizing, you each have absolute veto power. This ensures that neither of you buys into an agreement you dislike. You want a win-win solution, not a win-lose one.

Systematically review and evaluate each of the alternatives you generated during your brainstorming. We usually put a check in front of options we both like, cross out ones either of us vetoes, and place a question mark in front of those we're unsure of. Again, the key here is to respect one another's absolute veto power. No eye-rolling, sighing, or arguing allowed.

Typically one or two alternatives will remain. If not, odds are good that somewhere along the line, somebody didn't feel heard. Incidentally, hard feelings can flare up at any point in the process. It's important to listen them down using Dynamic Listening as soon as they occur, for a resentful negotiator is a resistant one who will likely sabotage the process.

If you vetoed all options, it's also possible that you didn't brainstorm enough alternatives. Consider returning to B if that's the case. There's no shame in taking a time-out as well. Just make sure that if you're the one suggesting it, you give your partner a specific time when you're willing to reconvene.

Assuming you were successful, however, pull together the agreed upon alternatives into a contract. Be clear and write down who does what, when, and how. Then give yourselves some leeway if you need to change the agreement later down the line.

*In our case, we stuck with our original plan. As expected, Cathy vetoed my hardline option that the kids pay their own way when we eat out, and I did the same on "going with the flow" and not looking at the Visa bill the following month.*

*As often occurs, we settled on a combination of several middle-*

*of-the-road options. We agreed on an overall budget figure and to go out for only one meal per day, but that I wouldn't comment on the cost.*

*The contract worked. We had almost no conflict the entire trip.*

Consider the ABCs of Harmonizing with other family members as well. It's not a difficult technique to explain, and you can also use it positively. For instance, we harmonized where to take our family vacation one year, and the kids eagerly joined in the process.

✳

**The C in the *ABCs of Harmonizing* is for choosing or contracting a solution to your midlife stalemate. Because you each have veto power, the agreement must be a win-win.**

✳

### Get Away for a State of the Union

To get the most out of Harmonizing, especially if you and your partner are negotiating a new marital, midlife contract, get away for the day or even the weekend. Make it a State of the Union, a special opportunity to reacquaint yourselves without the usual interruptions.

First, separate for an hour or two to clarify your thoughts and feelings about who you are as individuals and where you want your relationship to go at this point in your life. Then try a Letter Exchange to kick off the A in the ABCs of Har-mo-nizing. It's an excellent way to address the state of your union.

Remember not to criticize your partner's letter, to listen, especially when your spouse becomes emotional, and to voice several positives for every negative. Try to view your mate as a romantic foreigner who happened to sit next to you on a long-distance flight. Be as courteous and attentive to your midlife partner as you would to that intriguing stranger.

Take a break before brainstorming. Have lunch, go for a walk, or make love. Being as you have all day, consider giving each other time to brainstorm individually before putting your lists of options together. Remember, it's okay to take a time-out if you run into trouble, but exit politely and specify a return time. When all else fails, listen, listen, listen.

After choosing or contracting, celebrate over a good dinner. Then set aside time for a State of the Union every year, preferably on your anniversary. Your ongoing intimate relationship deserves it.

❋

**To renew your relationship at midlife, spend a day or weekend away for a special State of the Union. Then you'll have ample time to harmonize differences that emerge over the years.**

❋

## When to Back Off Rather Than Push for Change

You've probably seen the "Serenity Prayer" made popular by Alcoholics Anonymous: "God, grant me the serenity to accept the things I cannot change, the courage to change the things I can, and the wisdom to know the difference."

Well, this certainly applies to marriage and midlife transition. When do you push for change, and when do you back off and let your spouse be the separate and unique individual he or she is?

Although there are no hard and fast rules here, we do have a suggestion that can help you develop "the wisdom to know the difference."

### Does My Partner's Behavior Really Affect Me?

One question to help you determine whether to speak up or hold your tongue is "Does my partner's behavior really affect me?" (This is also useful when deciding whether to correct your kids, according to Tom Gordon in *Parent Effectiveness Training*.)

Consider the following example. If you light up a cigarette and your partner says, "You really shouldn't smoke, because it's not healthy," what's your reaction? If you're a smoker, odds are good that you'll get defensive. Why? Because you feel it's none of your mate's business. And you'd be right; after all, it's *your* body.

But notice what happens if your spouse says, "I wish you wouldn't light up, because I'm not feeling very well, and the smoke might make me gag." You're more likely to comply, because you see how your behavior affects your mate, tangibly and concretely.

Most cases of midlife change often have significant effects on a relationship, like if your partner pulls away sexually or gets more involved at work. The trick is to voice accurately how your mate's behavior impacts on you.

If you criticize your spouse for working too many hours, for instance, your partner might feel you're trying to control him or her. But if you share how lonely you are, your mate might be more open to receiving your message.

In any event, if you answer no to the question "Does my partner's behavior really affect me?" consider changing your self-talk. An alteration in your marital midlife expectations might rebalance your relationship.

❋

**When you're uncertain whether to back off or push for marital change, ask yourself, "Does my partner's behavior really affect me?" If it does, directly and concretely, tell your mate how.**

❋

*Intimacy and Independence: Beyond the Battle for Control*

Perhaps the most common and difficult challenge for relationships at any stage is balancing time together with time apart. In fact, when researchers compared key areas of marital conflict, everything from kids, sex, and money to in-laws and time and attention, how much time you spend with your partner was near the top of the list at every stage of the study.

Being "two together" is especially challenging at midlife, because the rules of the game are again up for grabs. When the kids leave, or when one of you changes careers, slows down, or retires, the balance of how much time you spend together as a couple versus how much each of you spends independently is again up for debate. And debate many of us do, as you saw earlier when Cathy began to pursue more separateness in our relationship.

Don't misinterpret your spouse's need for space as a personal rejection of you, however. Also, when your partner shares his or her thoughts and feelings, avoid personalizing the discussion. It's not necessarily about you. Cathy wasn't tired of our marriage; she was excited about her new sense of freedom now that the nest was emptying.

This can be especially sensitive when husbands retire. As one woman in her early fifties put it: "Now he expects to control me twenty-five hours a day." Women, particularly, often value their independence at midlife. Husbands would be well advised to cut their wives more slack during their middle and later years and not take it personally when their spouses head out the door for friends, new careers, or community activities.

❋

**Balancing intimacy and independence is particularly challenging at midlife. Women, especially, increasingly value their autonomy. Don't take your partner's push for separateness personally.**

❋

### *Let There Be Spaces in Your Togetherness*

Whether you're male or female, avoid the temptation to mold your partner into who *you* think he or she should be. Your spouse is a separate human being and not a vehicle to meet your needs. This is easier said than done, for we tend to grow territorial and possessive after many years of marriage.

It's one thing to *ask* your partner to fulfill your needs as you negotiate a new midlife contract; it's another to *expect* or *de-*

*mand* things. The writer Kahlil Gibran wrote in his classic *The Prophet* that there should be "spaces in your togetherness." He ended his words of wisdom about marriage with this:

*And stand together yet not too near together;*
*For the pillars of the temple stand apart,*
*And the oak tree and the cypress grow not in each other's shadow.*

# PART FOUR

# The Unique Challenges of Marriage at Midlife

*

Married couples are apt to find themselves in middle age, high and dry in an outmoded shell, in a fortress which has outlived its function. What is one to do— die of atrophy in an outstripped form? Or move on to another form, other experiences?

—Anne Morrow Lindbergh

CHAPTER 8

# Rekindling Your Sexual Relationship

*As a rule, women would like to devote as much to foreplay
and the sex act as men would like to devote to foreplay,
the sex act, and building a garage.*

—Dave Barry

The only time he ever touches me is when he wants sex," Janet complained, echoing the sentiments of many midlife wives. She missed how Roger used to glance at her over the dinner table to tell her she was attractive and loved. "I knew something was wrong," she continued, "when I realized that the last time we made love was two months ago, and that was when we spent a weekend away."

Now the only time Roger kissed her was on his way out the door, and that was just a quick peck on the cheek. He watched television late into the evening and often came to bed after she was asleep. Janet missed cuddling with him. Most of all, she missed feeling cared about and special.

For his part, Roger was bored with the routine of their sex life. He also didn't want to start something, only to have Janet say she was tired. "She used to get excited when I touched her," he said sadly. "Now she nods off as soon as her head hits the pillow."

Roger also worried that he might not get an erection ever since he had a problem a few months earlier. "Even if I did, my back might go out. That's the only thing stiff in the morning these days," he said, laughing halfheartedly. Although his erections were more hit than miss, they weren't as firm as they used to be.

Welcome to midlife! Besides the occasional erection problem, wrinkles come out of nowhere, waistlines expand, and hairlines recede. Your friends appear old, while the cop that pulls you over looks like a kid. Worse yet, he calls you sir or ma'am, and means it. Attractive waiters and waitresses treat you like Mom or Dad rather than flirt with you, while jokes about midlife increasingly hit home and grow darker with each decade.

But as the second half of life takes on new meaning physically, psychologically, and spiritually, it truly can be a time of sexual renewal, deeper intimacy, and emotional flowering. There are pearls in this supposed dustbin, if you know where to look and how to search for them. Bright among them is the increased ease and comfort you can find with your partner and your body as you explore a new and more satisfying dimension to your sexual relationship.

❉

**As your marriage loses novelty and your body its youthful vigor, midlife opens a previously unseen window through which you glimpse the potential for a truly intimate relationship.**

❉

## The Five Mistaken Beliefs About Midlife Sexuality

You've probably heard it said that your most important sexual organ is not between your legs, but between your ears. Sex is definitely one area where what you think affects how you feel. Those expectations become progressively important as you grow older. They influence performance, and more important, they alter your level of sexual satisfaction.

Five key mistaken beliefs or "shoulds" put undue pressure on your sexual relationship at midlife. Like dark clouds, they block out the love and joy that come from giving pleasure to your partner. Dissipate those dysfunctional assumptions, and you can rekindle the warmth and reignite the passion of your intimate relationship.

### *Mistaken Belief #1: Sex Should Always Be Lustful, Romantic, and Loving*

The bad news about an ongoing intimate relationship is that it gets old. You may not feel as lustful or romantic, for instance, as you did when you first explored each other sexually. You know the terrain, and there are fewer surprises.

The good news, however, is that with maturity and good communication, your level of sexual exploration can deepen. It can also be more honest. Being mature means having the courage to be who you are, not who you think you should be.

This is true across the board, but it most certainly includes your sexuality.

First, be honest with yourself. Then, be honest with your partner. Be realistic and flexible with your expectations as well. If you're in the mood for a "quickie" rather than the whole nine yards of lengthy foreplay and mutual orgasm, for instance, let your partner know early on.

After a long day at the office, you or your mate might not have the energy or the desire to "work" at your sexual relationship. In fact, studies show that the most common reason couples don't have sex is exhaustion. So don't make sex a second job. If you do it lovingly and positively, you can reassure your partner and save both of you a lot of unnecessary work and frustration.

❋

**Corrected Belief #1: Don't expect you or your partner to always be lustful, romantic, or loving. Rather than fake it, be honest with yourself and your spouse. Often a "quickie" will suffice.**

❋

*Mistaken Belief #2: Sexual Satisfaction Depends on Performance*

Young lovers assume that if they push the right buttons and perform the correct sequence of genital gymnastics, they and their partners will be sexually satisfied. While that's true to a certain extent, it becomes especially less significant at midlife, when your capacity and willingness to open up and connect emotionally become more important.

In the end, like the rest of life, you get what you give. The more vulnerable and present you are sexually, the more turned on, excited, and satisfied your spouse becomes. This isn't a matter of technique; it's a function of your maturity and your courage to strip naked psychologically under the penetrating gaze of your partner.

The ecstasy is in the union, the merging of souls. You won't get there planning your next move or worrying about what your spouse thinks of you. You get there by letting go, by abandoning yourself to the dance of intimacy.

We see this frequently with erection problems. If the cause is not physical, and it usually isn't during the early middle years, it's the worry that perpetuates the dysfunction. Both partners are focused on whether the penis will erect or not.

It's like trying to fall asleep. The more effort you put into it, the worse it gets. The trick is in the abandonment. For when a man loses himself in the passion of the moment, the natural wisdom of his physiology pumps blood into his penis. Sex happens. You don't "make" it happen; you get out of the way and allow it to do the voodoo it does so well.

❋

**Corrected Belief #2: Money can't buy you love; neither can performance. Sexual intimacy, especially at midlife, depends more on emotional intimacy and your courage to be open and honest.**

❋

*Mistaken Belief #3: Men Are Animals and*
*the Only Ones Interested in Sex*

Men underestimate a woman's sexual desire because they don't understand it. A man's sexual universe centers on the "big bang" theory of a quick and explosive orgasm. A woman's is a slow expansion of accumulated caresses and prolonged emotional exploration.

Both are interested in sex, but it's two different kinds of sex with vastly different languages, customs, and rhythms. Our culture drums some of those rhythms into our infant brains as soon as we are put to sleep on our first pink or blue pillowcases. Biology also primes the pump with divergent hormones and body parts as different as bowls and spears.

It's a cruel joke, and we are left scratching our heads in wonder and confusion as men are eager for penetration before women are emotionally prepared or sexually lubricated. A man is ready to "perform," but how athletic he is in bed is far less important to his wife than how he communicates that he wants to be there with her.

The trick is to understand the language of the other sex. The good news is that by midlife, we are not only older, but often wiser. We recognize and accept, albeit somewhat begrudgingly, many of these gender differences.

We are also less likely to imitate such cultural caricatures as Ken and Barbie, the Marlboro Man, or the latest anorexic fashion model. Men frequently aren't as afraid to be sexually tender or passive. Women may experiment with taking the initiative, especially after children leave the nest.

Biologically, even hormonal differences lessen. The percentage of the male hormone testosterone increases for some women as their estrogen level drops, which increases their sexual desire. Although menopause does put many women on "pause," they often become more sexually active afterward.

On the other side of the aisle, men meet them halfway. Because erections are slower to come by at midlife, sex includes more fondling and caressing before penetration. The good news for both sexes is that the chasm between men and women is bridged somewhat during their middle years.

❋

**Corrected Belief #3: Men aren't the only ones interested in sex. Women are too, but the language is different. At midlife, both genders meet halfway as physical and psychological needs change.**

❋

## Mistaken Belief #4: A Sexual Lull Means You Have a Problem

Are you satisfied sexually with your relationship? According to the research, most couples aren't. But that lull in your sex life doesn't necessarily mean you have a marital problem.

One study, for instance, found that 90 percent of most happily married couples have less-than-perfect sex lives during their middle years. They were happy despite the fact that over one-third of the men in the study ejaculated prematurely and nearly half the women had difficulty reaching orgasm.[1]

Conclusion? You don't need great sex to be happily married. It's how you talk to yourself about your sexual relationship that counts. Marital satisfaction depends more on how you perform inside your head than on your bed. As Hamlet says: "There is nothing either good or bad, but thinking makes it so."

Not only is your self-talk important, but how you talk to your partner is also essential. Other studies show that couples who communicate poorly are more likely to suffer ongoing conflict when sexual difficulties inevitably arise compared to couples with good communication skills.

Whether you experience a lull in your sexual desire sometimes depends on if you're male or female. Women often are affected by hormonal and family changes, for instance. While the birth of new children, teenagers roaming the house at all hours, and career stress can challenge both of you, such stress is more likely to influence sexual desire for you wives.

❦

**Corrected Belief #4: Don't let sexual lulls discourage you. It's how you talk to yourself and your partner about them that either perpetuates a problem or helps you pass through it.**

❦

### *Mistaken Belief #5: It's All in Your Head*

While many sex problems are triggered by stress, poor communication, or change within the family, some are due to physical causes. Take menopause, for instance. If you're female, even the *shape* of your body goes through a midlife transition. You gain weight just by looking at food, lose your rear end, and find your breasts down to your belly button. You also may get irritable and depressed, rise before the sun, or suffer hot flashes and memory loss.

A drop in estrogen can cause pain during intercourse, as vaginal fluids dry up and the walls of your vagina grow thinner. So don't be surprised if it takes longer to get aroused or lubricated. It's also par for the course if you feel self-conscious or undesirable because of the weight you've put on your midriff or bottom.

If you're male, you notice similar changes. Your waistline, like your wife's, is also expanding. You're not as strong in midlife as you used to be, and it takes longer to limber up. The force and frequency of your desire for sexual release declines as well. For instance, men who masturbated or had sex on a daily basis are now content with once or twice per week.

Midlife also raises progressively more anxiety and fewer erections. It takes you longer to achieve one, and the second erection might take several hours, rather than a few minutes. The force and amount of your ejaculation may decrease as well.

You also gradually lose your physical ability to respond visually to a sexual stimulus. Which means you're not as likely to get a hard-on simply by watching an attractive woman. This also means that your wife might need to lend a hand, so to speak, or arouse you orally; just looking might not be enough to excite you. You may need, dare it be said, *foreplay.*

If you are beyond foreplay and need Viagra or other medical assistance, keep in mind that your relationship may need some adjusting as well, especially if you've abstained sexually for a while and now suddenly want to jump back in bed again.

Whether you're male or female, these physical decreases in desire or performance also can be misinterpreted by your partner as a lack of caring. If your marriage is barely managing to get by already, such misunderstandings can tip the scale and throw your sexual relationship into dysfunction. Sometimes that can begin a slow, permanent decline. Best to talk things over or seek professional help early.

❋

**Corrected Belief #5: Changes in your sexuality at midlife aren't all in your head. Hormonal and other physical transitions, like menopause, can affect your sexual relationship significantly.**

❋

## Sexual Desire

Gary was a successful attorney with all the toys money could buy, but he felt like the forgotten runt of the litter, always on the outside. "The kids get it all," he argued, as if presenting his case before a jury. "There's never anything left for me."

His wife, Karen, felt guilty as accused. "I know he needs me, but after teaching all day, and then dinner and the kids at night, he's right—there's nothing left." Karen suffered from what is probably the most common enemy of sexual desire during the middle years—exhaustion. She also didn't feel close enough to be sexually open or vulnerable with Gary. This emotional distance contributed to their lack of sex as well.

Gary and Karen are like many midlife couples who struggle with a discrepancy in sexual desire. Although an increasing number of wives complain that their husbands have low sexual desire, ordinarily it's the husband who wants more frequency and variety.

In addition to exhaustion, emotional distance, and typical gender differences, reawakened ghosts of earlier sexual abuse can also dampen sexual desire. So can the temporary stress of such midlife changes as new children, career moves, and physical illness.

❋

**Sexual desire can be affected by exhaustion, differing
gender expectations, and emotional distance.
Previous sexual abuse and midlife changes, like
physical problems, can also take a toll.**

❋

### Exhaustion

With the increase in dual-career midlife couples, Gary and Karen are more the rule than the exception. It's hard to feel romantic when you work long days and then prepare dinner and supervise homework most evenings. By the time you hit the sheets, who's got the energy for anything other than a good book or staring at the ceiling for a few minutes before dozing off?

To prevent exhaustion from drying up your sexual desire, we suggest four things.

1. *Be realistic with your expectations*. If you're midlife, mid-family, and mid-career, don't expect frequent fireworks midweek. Most studies peg the average frequency for intercourse at about once per week. Be realistic, and consider anything more a bonus.

2. *Exercise*. If you have an hour for lunch, pack a yogurt, bagel, and apple, and either swim, jog, or hit the gym for forty minutes. Not only will you reduce stress and feel better about your body, studies show that exercise increases sexual desire for both males and females. It also helps with erection difficulties.

3. *Don't lose your marriage amid the demands of family life*. That goes double for your sexual relationship. Declare family time over at 9 P.M., for instance. Young kids are to be in bed with lights out by then. If you have teenagers, put them on notice that *you're* in bed by that hour and not to be disturbed. This gives you time to unwind, read, cuddle, and perhaps even have sex.

4. *Set aside a regular night out for your relationship*. Friday or Saturday is usually best. It's okay to meet friends, but save at least the first hour or so for just the two of you. When you're away from family, fax, and phone, you're more likely to unwind and enjoy each other. To further rekindle your sexual desire, check into a hotel for a weekend evening every few months.

Your sexual relationship during your middle years is part of the foundation for an ongoing successful marriage. Make it a priority by setting aside the time and energy it deserves.

❋

**Don't let exhaustion drain away your sexual desire. Be
realistic midweek, but end family time by 9 P.M.,
exercise, and get away for evenings and nights out.
Make intimacy a top priority.**

❋

*Men and Women Often Differ on Frequency and Variety*

You have to be careful defining what low sexual desire is and
who has it. For instance, remember that marvelous scene in
*Annie Hall*, one of Woody Allen's earlier movies, where he
complains to his therapist about Diane Keaton's low sexual
desire? He wonders aloud if she has a problem because she
wants sex so infrequently.

The camera then pans to a similar therapy session with
Keaton and her analyst. She suggests that Allen may have a
problem because he wants sex so often. We laugh, because
they're talking about the exact same thing, but from radically
different viewpoints.

We also laugh because most of us identify with them as
males or females. It is usually the husband who presses for
more frequency and variety, and it is typically the wife who is
accused of low sexual desire. If this is true in your relationship,
be careful not to buy into defining yourself as "dysfunctional,"
especially if you're the one accused of low sexual desire.

For instance, rather than a "cure" for *low* arousal, imagine
the following headline: NEW DRUG FOUND TO REDUCE PROB-
LEM OF HIGH MALE SEXUAL DESIRE. As you can see, one

person's dysfunctionally low sexual desire is another's pathologically high one.

Keep in mind, however, that in a growing number of relationships, the reverse is true; a substantial minority of wives complain that their husbands aren't interested. From jobs to sex, women have become progressively freer in Western society to explore a wider range of options across the board.

Many of today's midlife women also came of age during the sexual revolution as well. For better or worse, free love, drugs, and contraceptives were few and far between only a generation earlier. Whereas many of their mothers and grandmothers were taught to endure and service a husband's sexual needs, today's women expect pleasure and satisfaction themselves.

Today's women also have more power. That, in turn, may affect your sex life, especially who abstains and who pressures whom for sex, according to one study. Researchers found that partners who saw themselves as having less power in their relationship were more likely to be the ones with lower sexual desire.

How old you are also influences your level of sexual desire. As we discussed earlier, men become less spontaneously aroused as they grow older. For women, it's often the reverse. Menopause rules out pregnancy, freeing a woman from the subtle but often omnipresent fear of conception. In addition, as her children leave she can shift from a more maternal identity to one of sexual partner or mate.

Regardless of your gender, however, if you're the one who wants more sex, beware of pressuring your partner. Remember: Nobody wins if the relationship loses. You may win the body, but lose the spirit, as a backlash of resentment inevitably seeps into the marriage.

Better to "underwhelm" your mate with more frequent expressions of low-key affection, like a nongenital hug from behind as your partner washes the dishes, or cuddle up close and hold hands as you watch TV together. Warm your spouse up, but then give your partner room to make the next move.

If you're the abstaining spouse, up your affection, but increase your communication too. Tell your partner that you *want* to feel more sexy, and that if he or she would back off, for example, you will do your part and initiate more contact. Let your mate know, however, that in order for you to regain your sexual desire, it's better if things proceed at a pace more comfortable for *you*.

For instance, if you hug your spouse and he gets an erection, that doesn't mean it needs immediate release. Many wives feel pressured at this juncture, which causes them to withdraw affection entirely for fear it will "raise the issue." The key here is to lessen the pressure on the abstaining partner by each of you meeting in the middle.

❋

**Usually husbands push for more sex, but wives often do too, especially at midlife. Don't pressure the abstaining partner, however. Up your affection and communication instead.**

❋

*Emotional Distance Can Escalate into Sexual Distance*

Besides being exhausted from teaching all day and coping with the kids at night, Karen didn't open up sexually with Gary in that earlier example because she didn't feel emotionally close to him. This was especially frustrating for Gary, as it is for many men, because sex was one of the few languages of intimacy he knew how to speak.

But the harder he tried, the further Karen withdrew. It was a vicious cycle, and not uncommon. "I try to get her into it," Gary said with great exasperation, "but no matter what I do, it doesn't work." Like many men, he labored under the mistaken belief that sexual satisfaction depended on performance.

Karen, however, misinterpreted his intentions. "I feel like I'm in bed with Napoleon," she complained. "When he touches my vagina, it feels like an invasion. I don't want to be conquered, damn it. I want to be loved." It was a classic sexual misunderstanding, and their lack of communication only deepened their dilemma.

The more techniques Gary employed to ignite his wife sexually, the more pushed around and prodded Karen felt. The more Karen withdrew emotionally, the more frenetic Gary became in his efforts to push the right button. The cycle only escalated. After a while, you had a husband turning cartwheels over his wife's body in bed, while his wife watched as if a spectator from the corner of the room.

Both had reason to react the way they did. But because no one communicated, this *folie à deux* kept gathering steam. By the time we saw them for sex therapy, each was convinced that the other didn't care.

Gary concluded that his wife couldn't possibly love him. Why else was she so distant when they had sex? Karen, on the other hand, thought that her husband was only interested in "getting his rocks off." Why else did he play her like a honky-tonk piano and with so little feeling?

Gary and Karen gradually started to communicate instead of assuming that they knew what the other thought or felt. As they talked with each other, they began to turn their sexual relationship around. Sex became a vehicle for intimacy, rather than a minefield separating two lonely combatants.

❋

**Emotional distance at midlife can increase sexual distance when you and your partner misinterpret each other's actions and intentions. Honest communication helps bridge that distance.**

❋

### Ghosts of Earlier Sexual Abuse Sometimes Resurface

Gary and Karen's sexual minefield set off explosions on another level as well. Old issues from childhood, previously disarmed and boxed away, were retriggered by the current marital crisis. This is often the case, especially in such a primitive and vulnerable area as sexuality.

Karen's sense of invasion when her husband touched her vagina was the same feeling she experienced when her grandfather sexually molested her at ten years old. This is not to say that her problem with Gary was all in her head, however; Gary indeed played his part in triggering her reaction. But ghosts of earlier sexual abuse can be reawakened, especially when the problem in the present matches an earlier episode.

Sometimes the trigger is an aspect of a partner's behavior, like when Gary invaded Karen's vaginal area too brusquely.

Other times it may be a setting or other circumstance, like the smell of a new cologne. Once it activates a repressed feeling or image, however, a partner's emotional reaction can kick into high gear.

Often, though, it's more subtle. Gary's mother, for instance, was a cold and distant woman. His mission in life was to find the love he never got as a child. He spent much of his young adulthood chasing women, eventually marrying the one with the biggest breasts he could find.

During his middle years, however, when "the kids got it all," Gary felt unloved and abandoned, much as he had felt when he was a little boy. His frenetic sex drive was fueled by his unmet needs from childhood. When Karen withdrew emotionally during intercourse, Gary sensed that he was performing a one-man show. His genital gymnastics, experienced by Karen as a hostile takeover, were his best efforts to gain affection.

Getting the sexual intimacy you want is a two-step process. First, it depends on you becoming more aware of your underlying needs and triggers. In Karen's case, for example, she first had to work through her earlier abuse. Until she did, it was difficult for her to lose control and be sexually vulnerable.

But she also had to voice her needs for security and safety. It helped when she was able to say, "I need you to go slower, otherwise I get nervous and shut down." She also learned to reinforce Gary when things were going right: "Thanks for being so gentle, honey. I love it when you go slow."

Likewise, Gary had to become more aware of his unconscious needs and feelings and then voice them effectively. It also helped that both Gary and Karen learned about each *other's* areas of sensitivity. That way, they were less likely to overreact and take things personally when the other partner was triggered by some underlying individual issue and became agitated or withdrawn.

❃

**When ghosts of earlier sexual abuse resurface, they can frighten and magnify how you feel and react sexually. Awareness and communication are the two key ghostbusters.**

❃

## Midlife Change Can Stress Your Sexual Relationship

Alex was referred by his urologist for sex therapy after a thorough exam ruled out any physical problems. There was nothing wrong with his marriage, but he was worried sick about his finances. "I don't know how I'm going to keep the business afloat and put my kids through school," he worried, "let alone provide for Anna later down the line. There's nothing wrong with me that $100,000 couldn't fix."

He was right. His problem wasn't sexual; it was financial. Since his shop flooded out during an El Niño storm four months earlier, Alex worked twelve hours a day, six days a week. And at night, he just wasn't up for anything other than worrying.

Although Alex's situation is a bit extreme, life delights in throwing you a curve now and then. Don't be surprised if it affects your sex life. Career or job changes typically add stress and sap energy, for instance. Lose your job, especially if you're male, and your libido may not be far behind.

There are other stresses that typically occur at midlife as well, such as taking care of older parents or having a rebellious teenager wade blindly into a torrent of sex and drugs. When you're twenty-five, you bounce back quicker. But at fifty, for instance, stress takes more out of you physically and sexually.

❉

**Midlife change comes in many forms, some of which can affect you sexually, such as financial anxiety, problems with adolescent or adult children, or aging parents who suddenly need help.**

❉

### *Physical Illness Can Dampen Sexual Desire*

An unfortunate side effect of midlife is more frequent illness and disability. Sudden or ongoing health problems can make it uncomfortable to move your body, and depression can crop up as a secondary consequence of chronic illness or pain. Don't expect your sex life to remain magically unaffected.

Back and knee injuries, diseases such as multiple sclerosis and diabetes, accidents, surgeries, cancer, and creeping arthritis can often scar you physically, affect how you move and look, and have an impact on you psychologically. Accompanying fatigue, stress, pain, or anxiety can lower your sexual desire and arousal as well.

Take anxiety, for example. It's difficult to let go sexually if you're worried that your back might go out. To prevent your partner from misinterpreting your hesitation or reluctance, open up and share your concerns. Remember, it takes courage to risk being vulnerable. Ask for what you need nonetheless. Assertive sending is critical if you want to maintain a vibrant sexual relationship when illness or disability strikes.

Assertive sending also will enable your spouse to adapt more readily to your physical limitations and to move or stimulate you with greater sensitivity. You might find too that sharing intimately beforehand can become an arousing part of foreplay itself.

Be more flexible regarding sexual positions and experiment with ones you haven't considered in the past. Be creative choosing the time of day as well. If you suffer from arthritis or an old back injury, for example, you might need time to stretch out and limber up before engaging in intercourse. Make your preparations part of your shared sex play. Don't wait too long, however, for as the day wears on, fatigue often sets in.

Some surgeries are more challenging than others because they affect your body image. Hysterectomies and breast surgeries, for example, can wound a woman's physical self-esteem. It takes considerable courage and reassurance before climbing back into the sexual bed again.

Chemotherapy and radiation also can reduce a woman's sexual desire and activity. Sensitive communication is essential during these difficult transitions, especially listening. Consider using the Emotional Barometer to listen your partner down when she is upset.

Listening is also critical with men as well. Medications, frequently prescribed for depression and heart disease, can discourage erections and retard ejaculation. After a heart attack or stroke, both you and your partner might fear another trip to the emergency room and unintentionally pull away from each other sexually.

In addition, husbands who become physically disabled often must cope with the psychological hurdle of being financially dependent upon their wives. This can be especially challenging for men who pride themselves on being the chief wage earner and provider. This wound to a man's confidence and self-image of financial prowess also can affect his sexual performance.

To cope with these challenges, ask your doctor for specific information on how your illness and medication can affect your sex life. Also, read up on medication side effects yourself. The *Physicians' Desk Reference* (*PDR*) is what your doctor consults, and it's available at your public library. Accurate information will help you and your partner develop realistic expectations and not take failures personally.

So will doing the four-step. Don't assume that your partner's sexual reluctance is about you, especially if your spouse is battling a back problem or recovering from a stroke.

Finally, make good use of those moments when you don't have pain, and develop a plan to enjoy the limited time when you're not preoccupied with your illness or disease.

❋

**Physical illness may affect your sexual desire at some point during midlife. Get accurate information, up your communication, and develop a flexible and realistic sexual routine.**

❋

# Affairs

When sexual desire dips dangerously low, extramarital affairs at midlife become more tempting. This was the case for Sheree after twelve years of marriage to Nick. "I needed to feel desired, and Nick hardly spoke to me anymore."

Nick was furious. "I worked my ass off building up the business, especially after the kids were born, and this is the thanks I get!" He couldn't believe his wife cheated on him, especially since she was the one who was usually too tired for sex.

But the pattern is not unusual, as an increasing number of wives refuse to settle for marriages of emotional distance and little passion. Although more than a third of husbands have at least one sexual partner outside of marriage, according to the Kinsey Institute, their wives are not far behind.

Why do affairs happen? What do you do after your spouse finds out? More important, how do you heal after an affair, and what can you do to prevent them?

## What Are Affairs?

Before we can answer those questions, we need to look at what affairs are to begin with. For openers, they almost always involve deception and a violation of trust, as one partner betrays either a spoken or assumed agreement to be faithful.

Sometimes they're flings or one-night stands. Often they're

triggered by circumstances, like being drunk while away at an overnight conference. These affairs typically lack emotional involvement and usually don't mean you're dissatisfied with your marriage. Although all affairs kick up more conflict than couples expect, the good news is that relationships usually heal more effectively after a one-night stand compared to other, more serious affairs.

Then there's the partner who engages in a *series* of one-night stands. Because the flings themselves avoid intimacy or involvement, they again are less serious. The repeated, unfaithful behavior, however, is a different story. As you might expect, couples who struggle with serial affairs are less likely to repair their relationship because trust is continually betrayed.

Also difficult are affairs that involve a high degree of emotional involvement. This was the case with Sheree and Nick. She became romantically attached to her lover over the course of several months. By the time the affair was discovered, Sheree was unsure which way to turn. She didn't want to destroy her marriage, but she cared deeply about her boyfriend.

In some long-term affairs, all three partners in the triangle have an unspoken agreement to continue the illusion and pretend the affair doesn't exist. Although this was not the case with Sheree and Nick, some couples decide not to rock the marital boat. Often it's done to protect the family during the middle years from the painful disruption of divorce. Such triangles are common in Europe but relatively rare in the United States.

❋

**More than one-third of all husbands have an affair, as do almost as many wives. How you repair your marriage afterward depends on how long the affair lasted and how intimate it was.**

❋

## *Why Do They Happen?*

Sheree's affair is a textbook example of why women have affairs. Her need to "feel desired" and her frustration with Nick's lack of communication are classic complaints.

Both are supported by a study of 150 mostly middle-aged women who had affairs outside marriage. All admitted that communication was a big factor. They also sought a more emotional relationship rather than sexual thrills.

Men, as we've said all along, are built differently. They frequently search out other women for sexual novelty and variety. This isn't always the case, however. Many men who feel distant and ostracized will seek intimacy as well as sex if they feel unloved at home.

Regardless of whether you're male or female, however, as you enter midlife, unfulfilled fantasies and expectations often feel more urgent as you sense time ticking away. Your desperation may deepen as you age. Viagra and other medications for erection difficulties have added new temptation to meet your needs outside of marriage as you increasingly recognize your spouse's limitations and the likelihood that he or she won't change much in years to come. You're more likely to feel restless during key times of marital stress or transition as well, like when children begin to leave the nest.

Beware, too, of boredom and taking your relationship for granted at midlife. And avoid putting all your energy into your children, your work, or yourself. They can isolate you from your partner and provide a dangerous breeding ground of loneliness and frustration that can precipitate an affair. Verbal or physical abuse can push you toward an affair as well. So can feeling emotionally neglected or abandoned, like when a spouse withdraws due to alcohol or drug use.

If you decide to end your marriage, however, don't have an affair as an excuse to exit. It's salt in the wounds for your partner, who is likely to be angry enough already because you instigated the divorce. Don't complicate the process further, especially if you have children.

*

**Women typically have affairs for communication and emotional intimacy, while men seek sexual novelty and variety. Both genders feel more desperate as time slips away during midlife.**

*

### What to Do When Your Partner Finds Out

Most people don't tell their partners about an affair until it's discovered. You might, however, feel so guilty about it that you confess to relieve your inner turmoil. Unfortunately, that usually starts more relationship turmoil than you anticipated.

Another reason you might spill the beans is to tell your

partner how angry and frustrated you've been with your relationship over the years. But it can also be a way to end your marriage if you know that your spouse won't be able to handle the betrayal. In addition, you might tell your partner about the affair as a way to justify why you think the marriage should be ended. Sometimes, however, exposing the truth can be an unconscious way to end the affair.

Regardless of whether you tell your partner or the affair is discovered by your spouse, if you want to heal your marriage, you must be willing to stop the affair, immediately and completely.

You also need to prepare yourself for a lengthy period of insecurity and anger on the part of your spouse. It often takes a year to heal the distrust, but the first few months are usually the most intense. Your immediate task is to listen and to answer your partner's many questions.

Studies show that men are more frequently threatened by the *sexual* aspects of a wife's affair, while women worry more about the degree of *emotional* intimacy experienced by a husband with his lover. So be prepared for questions and anxiety along those lines in particular. Expect some crossover, however, as many wives also will want sexual details, and husbands frequently ask about emotional attachment as well.

✻

**Once the affair is discovered, it's important to break off all contact, listen patiently, and answer your partner's many questions. Be patient, especially during the first few months.**

✻

## *How to Heal After an Affair*

After the initial crisis, prepare yourself for a year of gradual re-building. How much will depend on the type of affair you had. Generally, it takes more patience than you expect, especially if you're the one who had the affair.

It's normal for your partner to ask a million questions, many of them over and over again. Answer them honestly, thoroughly, and patiently. It will help your spouse calm an unsettling whirlwind of painful feelings and questions. Don't forget to use the listening skills we talked about in chapter 5.

Express sincere remorse. Your partner will need to hear periodically how sorry you are that he or she was hurt. Reassure your spouse regularly of your love and commitment as well.

Despite your best efforts to be patient, your mate's insecurity will get old after a few months. Remind yourself that your partner is doing the best he or she can, and that if you were in your partner's shoes, you might have as difficult a time too. Give your spouse the benefit of the doubt.

Give your partner information as well about where you're going and who you'll be with. Be dependable. Call if you're going to be late. What may be a few minutes to you will feel like an hour in purgatory for your partner.

If your spouse was the one who had the affair, control your urge to blame and retaliate. As we talked about in chapter 6, be assertive rather than aggressive, and get below your anger when possible. You're more likely then to get the listening and reassurance you need.

Challenge irrational or negative thinking as well before it blossoms into self-blame and anxiety. You can also calm yourself down with deep breathing, meditation, prayer, and exercise.

Both you and your partner may need to share responsibility for mismanaging your marriage before the affair. Whoever chose to betray the other is still responsible for breaking such sacred vows as commitment and trust. But both of you may need to examine how each of you lowered the level of intimacy in your relationship.

If you were the one who was betrayed, getting to forgiveness will be one of your biggest hurdles. Remind yourself that by this stage in your life and marriage, you too made mistakes and unintentionally hurt your partner. Choose to forgive and to let go of bitterness.

Decide to grow from the experience as well. As Nietzsche wrote: "That which does not kill me, makes me stronger." That applies to relationships also; that which does not kill *us* can make *us* stronger too.

❋

**If you're the spouse who cheated, be patient, answer your partner's repeated questions, and be dependable. Healing from an affair usually takes longer than you expect, often a full year.**

❋

### How to Prevent an Affair

There are several steps you can take to prevent affairs from happening in the first place. To begin with, review with your partner what you each mean by fidelity at midlife. Is it okay to flirt, for example? How about friendships with the opposite sex? Lunch with a coworker?

Then use the communication skills you read about in earlier chapters. If you feel threatened when your partner grows too close to a member of the opposite sex, get below your anger and voice your anxiety, for instance. If your spouse becomes defensive, listen down your mate's emotional pressure or defensiveness.

Review your own boundaries at midlife as well. We strongly recommend that you make two conscious decisions up front. First, decide now not to be in two beds at the same time. And second, don't allow yourself to get too close to a potential target to begin with.

Besides renewing boundaries with your partner and yourself, put time and energy into your marriage. Prioritize your relationship with the same intensity and perseverance that you would with a customer or client. Share your thoughts and feelings, but also your hopes and dreams. This is especially important for you husbands. According to the research, it may be the single most important thing you can do to prevent your wife from having an affair.

Remind yourself to be positive, too, rather than focus on your partner's shortcomings or what you would like to change about your mate. This particularly applies to you wives. Don't lose the forest for the trees and overlook steadfastness and commitment for how much television is watched or where your husband throws his dirty socks. Remember why you fell in love with your partner to begin with, and give voice to that appreciation.

That includes the bedroom as well. For one of the best ways

to prevent affairs, especially by husbands, is to reignite your sexual relationship.

❃

**Talk may be cheap, but it can prevent your wife from having an affair, according to the research. Wives, up your positives and your sexuality. Both of you win if you prioritize your marriage.**

❃

## Rekindle Passion with the Four C's of Sexual Arousal

When you're courting, it's "any room in the house" sex. During midlife, it's only in the bedroom. And for older couples, it's hallway sex: that's when you pass each other in the hall mumbling, "Screw you, screw you" to each other.

Well, if you want to avoid becoming the butt of that joke, practice what we call the Four C's of Sexual Arousal: creativity, courage, communication, and courtship.

### *Creativity Keeps Your Relationship Forever Young*

First, be creative. Don't become the victim of routine. A steady diet of anything is boring after a while. Spice up your relationship by trying different positions or places to have sex, like the bathtub, the floor . . . or even the hallway.

Don't underestimate oral sex either, especially as you grow older. It will help stimulate your husband and can lubricate wives during their middle years and beyond. If you've hesitated to try it, talk to your partner about your fears and take small steps at first. Bathing and flavored oils may help get you started. Also, ask your partner to lie on his or her back so you feel more in control. It's okay to kiss or gently lick your partner, for instance, rather than stick his penis into your mouth.

Keep in mind that what turns you on, however, often depends on whether you're male or female. For men, it's usually something concrete, like a new sexual position or erotic nightie. Few things will bring a man greater joy than being in bed with a wild and adventuresome woman. Be that woman, and you dramatically ratchet up your sexual relationship and rejuvenate your marriage in general at midlife.

In order to be the seductress, however, you'll need to be warmed up considerably beforehand. Tell your partner what you need. Do it positively and early, before you become resentful. It's not only in *your* best interest to let your spouse know what you need, but it's ultimately in *his* best interest as well. Help him turn you into the tigress he longs for. Tell him what you need and show him how to excite you.

If men hunger for variety, women typically long for romance, emotional connection, and slow, prolonged foreplay. Creative sex begins long before you hit the bedroom door. Bring her flowers, kiss her for no apparent reason, and ask her about her day. Being creative means being romantic. Women need to feel loved before they can feel sexy.

Show her love in the bedroom as well. Go slowly, and drive

her wild with extended kisses and caresses. If you haven't spent much time stimulating her clitoris either manually or orally, now's the time to begin. Rather than rush toward orgasm, linger in passionate foreplay. Arouse her to the point where she *wants* to move ahead. Once she's hot enough, you won't have to push her. She'll take *you* there, breathlessly.

❋

**The first C of sexual arousal is creativity. Men love concrete gestures like new sexual positions and erotic clothing. Women relish romance, emotional connection, and extensive foreplay.**

❋

### *Find the Courage to Ask for What You Need*

At midlife you need the courage to stand by your needs and desires. Participating passively in sexual positions and experiments breeds resentment and creates distance between you and your partner.

That was the problem for Debra. Like many wives, Debra believed that if she didn't acquiesce when her husband wanted sex, he would find release in the arms of another woman. "I know this sounds old-fashioned," she admitted sheepishly, "but I'm afraid that if I don't spread my legs when he needs me, he'll find another woman who will."

Debra's lack of courage was the chief reason she had turned off sexually in an otherwise successful eighteen-year marriage with her husband Darrell. He was also frustrated by her passive compliance, for although he didn't understand why she was resentful, he nonetheless felt her distance in bed.

When Debra found her courage, their sexual relationship improved, especially after she voiced her need for more foreplay. "I need to be more turned on, honey," she said softly. Then she added the following positive suggestion in the guise of an observation: "You know how you drive me wild when you caress my clitoris." As Darrell backed off on frequency and picked up his foreplay, he and Debra gradually rekindled their sexual relationship at midlife.

It's important, however, to *remind* your partner periodically of what you need. Just because you told your partner several years ago that you needed more foreplay, for instance, doesn't mean he'll remember. In fact, if it's physically important to you but not to him, it's normal for him to forget. Courage, risk-taking, and vulnerability aren't one-time occasions; they're for the life of your sexual relationship.

❀

**The second C to rekindle your sexual passion is courage. To prevent resentment from breeding distance, voice your needs early, and remind your partner of them periodically.**

❀

## Be Clear and Direct in Your Communication

After you find your courage, you then need to communicate clearly and effectively. Besides enhancing intimacy, communication helps resolve sex problems.

This is true even when they're triggered by physical conditions, like some erection failures, for instance. "Often lack of communication," writes noted sex researcher Helen Singer Kaplan, "helps to perpetuate a dysfunctional sexual system and to escalate an existing problem." Good communication, however, can help you hurdle many of those sexual impasses that crop up during your middle years.

It clarifies the what, when, where, and how of sexual engagement. Tell your partner what feels good and what doesn't, for instance. Be positive, but don't hesitate to guide your partner's hand when necessary. If grunts and groans don't get your point across, use your words, as Mother used to say.

Be sensitive to differences in your communication styles. You might be more affected sexually by work stress or relationship conflict than your partner is, for example. This is more likely to happen to women, but not necessarily so, especially during later midlife. For many, it's difficult to have good sex when you don't feel good about yourself or your relationship.

❋

**The third C is communication. It's normal at midlife to hit ruts in your sex life. With good communication, you can recontract a new, more exciting, and fulfilling sexual relationship.**

❋

### Renew Your Courtship at Midlife

Think back to how much time and effort you put into wooing your spouse when you first met. How you dressed up, bought flowers, or perhaps listened attentively. You went the extra mile to impress your partner, and it worked. Your soon-to-be mate fell in love with you and was sexually excited by your touch, maybe even your voice.

Some of that was due to the mystique and novelty of a new relationship. But the attention and effort you put into courtship also played a huge role. And why wouldn't it? Does your business or career succeed without effort? Would your children feel loved and cared for if you didn't prepare meals, tuck them in at night, or console them when they were troubled or upset?

Success rarely happens without sustained effort and ongoing attentiveness. Why should your marriage be any different? The bottom line here is that if you want your relationship to work, you have to work at it and make it a priority.

Put sex in your schedule, for instance. If that sounds too regimented, consider that when you courted, you set aside time to go on dates together, didn't you? Rather than deaden the experience, scheduling a date heightened your excitement because you looked forward to it with romantic and sometimes erotic anticipation.

Even if you don't engage in intercourse, you give yourselves a valuable opportunity for some tender and pleasurable contact. If you put one-fourth the energy into romance and seduction that you did when you dated, the effort and communication alone will serve as powerful aphrodisiacs. So does the assumed message, "I want to be with you and am willing to set aside my time for you."

✻

**When you courted, the last C to rekindle sexual arousal, you primped, seduced, and lavished special attention on your partner. Set aside similar time and energy again at midlife.**

✻

The sexual dance as an expression of love and intimacy can be a powerful means to recharge your marriage at midlife, but you won't get there by following a rule book. Be creative and have the courage to voice your personal feelings and individual sexual needs.

*Think* with creativity and courage as well. Middle age can mean attractive, confident, and sexy. Finally, renew your communication and courtship to reignite the passion and intimacy of your sexual relationship at midlife.

### CHAPTER 9

# The Sandwich Generation: Exiting Children and Aging Parents

Home is the place where, when you have to go there,
they have to take you in.

—Robert Frost

Remember the image of the mobile and how individual or family change disrupts the delicate balance between you and your spouse? It happens when kids enter a marriage, and it happens when they exit as well.

Take pieces away, like when your teenagers assert their independence and leave home, for instance, and the mobile again swings wildly out of balance. This transition begins when the kids hit their midteens, but continues through their early twenties, and it can throw chaos into a marriage at midlife.

Besides kids growing up and moving out, another mobile buster begins to emerge from the other end of the family spectrum. Your aging parents become increasingly dependent on you for physical and emotional support. That's why couples in this in-between stage are called the "sandwich generation."

Besides being sandwiched between children and parents, you may be under considerable financial pressure as well, as couples during their middle years typically shoulder heavy workloads, retirement plans, mortgage payments, and large debts.

## Adolescence: The Nest Begins to Empty

This was the case for Gayle and Patrick when their three kids entered adolescence and started to leave the nest. Along with the mortgage, they now had to set aside money every month for college tuition. It was also during this time that Patrick's father had a disabling stroke.

The biggest challenge, however, was Gayle's. A self-described "control freak," she found letting go of her children especially difficult. Jeremy, the youngest, tried to reassure her during a family therapy session. "We still need you, Mom," he told her, "just not in the same way." But Gayle couldn't hear it. Her fear of losing control over her children was over-whelming.

Although the trigger for Gayle's anxiety was when the kids became increasingly independent, the powder for this volatile season of transition was loaded long before. Growing up with an unpredictable and sometimes explosive alcoholic father left Gayle needing a lot of control in her life.

"Because I never knew what to expect, I learned to be both on guard and on edge," she told us. "I also learned to take things into my own hands." This worked well during the early years of her marriage, however, as Patrick loved how independent and competent Gayle was and how she juggled both her job and the kids with considerable skill.

The challenge came when the kids hit adolescence and sought more independence and control over their lives, separate from their parents. "I feel like I did when I was six years old," Gayle blurted out anxiously. "Every time I come home, I never know what I'll find! Either the kids are not doing what they're supposed to, or they're not there period."

Her children caused anxiety even in her dreams. The night before our session, Gayle dreamt that her eighteen-year-old daughter was pregnant and her seventeen-year-old son turned up HIV positive. Gayle grew less anxious and more angry as the session continued. "I'm expected to pick up the pieces, only I can't find them, and when I do, I can't fit them back together again!"

Her marriage was in pieces as well. Patrick depended on Gayle to be in charge and to take care of details. He wasn't used to her falling apart, and he wasn't very sympathetic either.

For Patrick, the chaos of the teenage years seemed normal. When he grew up, kids were always coming and going, fighting, getting into trouble, and stretching the limits. That's what teenagers do, as far as he was concerned. He remembered arguing with his parents about the rules and expectations, even winning on occasion. From his point of view, Gayle was making a big deal out of something that seemed normal.

Patrick also felt frustrated by the pressure this put on their marriage, especially the increased demands on him. They were particularly irritating on the nights he came home late after helping his parents with his father's recovery from his stroke.

The kids used to go to Gayle when they had problems or needed things, and although Patrick felt involved, he hadn't felt overwhelmed.

"Things sure are different now," he remarked. "The kids are all over me about Gayle as soon as I come home. 'Mom doesn't trust us. Mom won't let us go out this Friday night after the game.' And then Gayle complains about the kids being out of control and hammers me for twenty minutes about being too soft on them!" Patrick was clearly disgusted. His once happy home was in turmoil, and he held Gayle responsible.

What Gayle and Patrick needed to hear was that this difficult time of transition was par for the course. Marriages as well as families change as kids enter, grow up, and eventually leave the nest. Gayle sensed, appropriately so, that things were changing dramatically, and this change frightened her. This was partly because of her personal issues regarding control, but also because anxiety is a typical response to change for many of us.

❋

**When your kids hit adolescence and leave the nest, the loss of control can trigger anxiety and family conflict. This can challenge your marital relationship during midlife as well.**

❋

Even though they didn't need to push away from an explosive, alcoholic father as she had, Gayle began to appreciate why her children needed to separate from their parents nonetheless. She started to respond with more empathy and compassion, as she acknowledged their journey to establish their own identities.

As Gayle let go of her children, her marriage freed up and moved ahead as well. This is a good example of how renewing your relationship during your middle years is often less a marital issue and more a function of how you or your spouse negotiates an important midlife transition as an individual.

Counseling helped the family better understand why the mobile was swinging wildly out of balance. It also enabled them to hear one another more clearly and to express their feelings in nonattacking ways.

The key, however, was when Gayle came to grips with the end of a major part of her midlife journey as a mother. She and Patrick were then free to explore new roads together as a couple.

## After the Kids Leave: The Empty Sandwich

One of the biggest challenges during your middle years is how to rekindle your relationship once your children leave the nest. This is also true for you second marriages and stepfamilies.

The mobile again dramatically shifts, and you are left dangling dangerously out of balance. Do you still have anything in common as a couple? you wonder. Your lives, once jointly wrapped around football games or dance recitals, begin to unravel.

Instead, you glance nervously at your spouse on Friday nights like a junior high kid on a dance floor. Do I ask her to dance? What if she doesn't want to? Or what if *my* feelings for *her* have changed, and I'd rather be out with my friends? More dangerous still, what if I'd rather be with another lover?

It's crucial during this time to remember why you came to-gether in the first place. Go through your picture albums and note why you fell in love with your partner. Ironically, it may be similar qualities today that now frustrate or irritate you. Challenge yourself, nonetheless, to see what it was that first attracted you.

✴

**After the children leave, rediscover what first attracted you to your partner. Look through old picture albums and challenge yourself to see the positives you saw back then.**

✴

### *Remind Yourself of Your Partner's Strengths*

One of Phyllis's first recollections of Todd was the expansive way he waved at her as they bicycled to meet for their first date. She liked his spontaneity and outgoing nature, perhaps because it reminded her of her father, who was a gregarious and boisterous man.

Now, however, all she sees is how loud and self-centered he is. True, those are the negative sides of his personality style. But if she can balance her negative thinking with the positives that were there when they first met, and may still be there now, she can change how she feels about Todd. Remember, what you choose to see influences how you think, and what you think creates how you feel. For example, rather than focus on Todd's loud behavior at the restaurant, if Phyllis focused on how he made the waiter laugh and how the tourists at the bar enjoyed learning about the area from her husband, she can begin to change the thoughts and conclusions she has about him. As Phyllis constructs this more positive image or impression of Todd, her respect and appreciation gradually rebuild.

It's like the bumper sticker EXPECT A MIRACLE. You tend to get what you look for. Expect your partner to be loud and self-centered, and that's likely what you'll see. But if you look for positive aspects of that same personality style, perhaps social charm or courage to risk sharing an unpopular political opinion, you're more likely to view your spouse differently.

✸

**Expect the positive, and you're more likely to see it. If you increasingly notice your partner's good points, you'll change how you think and feel about your relationship.**

✸

## Get Away Together for a State of the Union

Besides changing how you talk to yourself, change how you talk to your partner. Make a commitment as a couple to rewrite a new marriage contract now that the kids are gone. Use either the Give and Take or the Letter Exchange we talked about in chapter 7 to guide your communication as you dialogue back and forth. It's best to get away from the house for the day or weekend to make it a special State of the Union.

First, give yourselves time alone as individuals to collect your thoughts about where you would like to go with your life now that the children are gone. After you each feel clearer about your hopes and goals for the future, which may take time to discover and clarify, listen to or read your partner's position. Don't criticize, however; keep it positive. When you review your partner's point of view, see your spouse as a man or woman at midlife, rather than as your husband or wife.

Look for common ground, but give your partner the freedom to pursue interests that you don't hold in common as well. For instance, if you both agree that you would like to travel more, develop a plan to do that as a couple. But if one of you wants to go into business while the other desires to attend church more regularly, give each other the room to be who you are as individuals. You would do no less for a good friend, so give your spouse the same courtesy and freedom. Besides being your marital partner, your mate is also an individual on a journey unique to him or her.

❋

**Spend a day or weekend away for a State of the Union to reevaluate your hopes and goals for the future. Be open, don't criticize, and allow for individual differences.**

❋

Too often we stop sharing how we feel because we don't know how, or we're afraid that our partner might judge or reject us. But to be companions at love, we need to find the courage to walk a new path, to overcome our vulnerability and fear of disappointment.

This is also the time to practice the communication skills you learned earlier. During a State of the Union, it's important to keep in mind that your partner may not have the same needs or goals as you. Be respectful of these differences. It's crucial if you're going to successfully renew your relationship at midlife.

### *Avoid the Nine Parent Traps of Relating to Adult Children*

As your marriage matures during your middle years, your relationship with your children changes. Trying to exert the same kind of control you once did can trigger conflict between you and your *kids*, and can also prove hazardous to your *marital* health.

1. *Don't overprotect your adult children from making the same mistakes you made.* It can damage your relationship with them, and that can cause marital tension as well.

2. *Let go of external control gradually over the years.* This will help the entire family get used to their emerging roles.

3. *Don't think of your adult children as extensions of yourself.* Putting that kind of pressure on your kids may make your spouse resentful.

4. *Develop an identity beyond being a parent.* Generate balance in your life with fulfilling activities, a good support system, or perhaps a new career.

5. *Let go of pressuring yourselves to put up a united front.* Swallowing your opinions isn't going to help your marriage.

6. *Don't criticize how you or your partner parented over the years.* Remember that we all make mistakes. You also did the

best you could at the time; otherwise, you would have done it differently.

7. *Be a supportive consultant rather than a critical boss who is avoided and resisted.* Becoming a good listener and a sought after mentor frees your marriage from the pressures of child rearing.

8. *Set clear limits.* Don't allow yourself to be manipulated or abused by your children. Although you'll be tested at first, your kids will eventually get the message, and your marriage will be stronger for it.

9. *Mind your own business.* It protects your relationship with your adult children, and they learn best from the consequences of their own behavior. Save your energy for your spouse. Don't waste it on losing battles.

## Aging Parents

The other slice of bread in the sandwich generation is coping with your parents as they grow older and become more dependent. They begin to need more from you physically, emotionally, or financially. Just as the kids empty the nest and you sense freedom around the corner, your parents increasingly take a bite out of your clock with greater demands on your time.

This can become especially burdensome for you wives, who usually assume the caretaker role. One study reports that nearly one of every five women in this country between forty and sixty-four years old provides several hours of help every week to either their or their husband's parents.[1]

Not only can the hours be stressful, reversing roles with your parents can be psychologically challenging as well. Add it all up, and it can weigh heavily on a marriage at midlife, whether you take care of older parents in your home, nearby, or long distance.

❖

**Nearly one of every five women at midlife helps an aging parent several hours every week. The additional burden can trigger conflict for a sandwich-generation couple.**

❖

### Dependent Parents Can Strain Your Marriage

Taking care of Mom and Dad can also challenge you and your marriage if you endured a troubled relationship with them during childhood. If you felt inadequate in your parents' eyes, for instance, that can compromise your ability to make difficult decisions regarding their day-to-day living and quality of life. In a similar fashion, how you got along with your in-laws over the years can complicate caretaking for a sandwich couple.

Bonnie and Stuart are a good example. She enjoyed the relationship she had with her mother now that she was in her middle years, but that wasn't the case growing up. As a child, Bonnie felt she could do nothing right for her mom. Bonnie had learned to be more assertive and self-confident during her twenties and thirties, however. Since they lived only half an hour apart, it was easy to get together, and her mother was appreciative of the time and attention Bonnie gave her.

Stuart, on the other hand, resented the time his wife spent with her mom. He remembered many nights after family get-togethers during the early years of their marriage when he would hold Bonnie as she cried herself to sleep after being hurt by her mother's criticism and insensitivity. He also remembered the disapproval Bonnie's mother showed him during the first ten years of their marriage.

Nonetheless, he worked hard at holding his tongue. This became increasingly difficult. Since his father-in-law's death, his mother-in-law dropped by every other evening. Stuart resented her taking advantage of Bonnie and their limited resources, but he felt powerless, for he knew how much this new relationship with her mother meant to Bonnie. After a few months, however, Stuart ran out of patience. The tension for this sandwich-generation couple finally boiled over into marital conflict.

If we return to our image of the mobile, Stuart and Bonnie's conflict as a couple should come as no surprise. Such family transitions are par for the course during midlife. The new balance between Bonnie and her mom was fine for the two women, but it disrupted the marital balance between Bonnie and Stuart.

Stuart felt like second fiddle to his mother-in-law. "This was supposed to be our time," he said, "now that the kids are gone and our life is less complicated." Besides his periodic explosions, he had withdrawn emotionally during the last few months.

Bonnie, for her part, felt caught in the middle. "Why can't he understand that I'm finally having a decent relationship with my mother?" She sensed that Stuart felt left out, but she couldn't appreciate how hurt and abandoned he felt. The more he withdrew, the more time she spent with her mother. It had become a vicious cycle by the time they sought therapy.

The turning point in their conflict came when they were able to hear each other's pain and perspective. As is typical in marital conflict, it wasn't that one of them was right and the other wrong. Stuart and Bonnie each had legitimate points of view; each was half right.

To make it all right, they first needed to hear and value the other half, the half they weren't hearing. Once they did, they were able to agree on a plan of action. The hard part, however, was really hearing and valuing what the other had to say.

❀

**A sandwich-generation couple can be thrown off balance
by the increased needs of a dependent parent.
The bottom line for resolving conflict is hearing and
valuing each other's position.**

❀

### Be Realistic with Your Expectations

Dealing with aging parents raises additional issues. First, your relationship with your mom and dad won't necessarily improve dramatically just because you now sacrifice time, energy, or financial resources to take care of them.

On the contrary, aging parents frequently become stuck in

their ways. This is partly due to experience, but often due to physical limitations as well. Increased aches and pains, like the "twinges in the hinges" that come from arthritis, can limit their ability to move about or feel comfortable in many situations.

For instance, when Gene and Renae had to take care of Gene's mom after she had hip surgery, her lack of mobility made it difficult for them to attend their daughter's basketball games. Often Gene would stay with his mom, while Renae went to the games. It didn't exactly create a marital crisis, but it deprived them of one of the few things they enjoyed doing together as a couple.

Older people also experience more losses. Your parents or in-laws will lose friends and family, their independence, even their ability to control their bladders. As a result, they often have less emotional and physical reserve.

Gene's mom, Ida, for instance, became more grouchy, intolerant, and demanding as her arthritis worsened over the years. This was particularly challenging for Gene, who had never felt valued or accepted by his mother, especially compared to his successful older brother. He had hoped that by taking care of his mother, she would finally realize what a good son he was.

Watching Gene's continual disappointment was even more frustrating for Renae. She hated the way Gene's mother belittled and discounted him. It was all she could do to maintain a civil relationship with her mother-in-law, especially as Ida became more intolerant and inflexible as she grew older.

❋

**Don't expect aging parents to be more appreciative
or accepting just because you now take care of them.
It's a difficult time for them too; they often feel
physically and emotionally exhausted.**

❋

### Duty Is in the Eye of the Beholder

How much stress you experience taking care of your aging parents is also influenced by why you do it to begin with as well as what your parents and spouse expect of you.

For instance, do you do it more out of obligation and duty or out of love and affection? According to a study in the journal *Psychology and Aging,* if you care for your aging parents because you love them rather than because you feel obligated, you're less likely to feel stress.[2] This is no small matter according to the study, for about half of us think of it more as a responsibility, while the other half do it primarily because of feelings of affection.

How you care for your mom and dad is also influenced by what they expect of you. Take Sandra's case, for example. When her mom, Alice, needed help, she expected Sandra to visit every day. That's what Alice's mom had expected of her a generation earlier. For Alice it was simple: Daughters take care of aging moms.

This put considerable pressure on Sandra and her husband, Kevin, because to oppose the party line meant treason and excommunication. Sandra loved her mother, but she didn't want to visit and care for her every day, as her mom had done for her own mother.

Sandra's quandary is not uncommon. Such unspoken rules of obligation and duty are often passed down from one generation to the next. Sometimes we follow the example of our parents in how they took care of their folks, as Sandra's mother had a generation earlier. But sometimes we don't, which is what Sandra chose to do.

When she was a young girl, she had seen her mother run ragged by her grandmother, often taking Alice away from her and her younger brother when she was needed at home. It left an impression on Sandra, who was determined not to do that to *her* family.

It was not easy disappointing her mother, for Alice equated daily visits with love. But Sandra used the Emotional Barometer technique we talked about in chapter 7, and eventually Alice was able to hear that her daughter still loved her, even though she deviated from the family model.

This also freed up Sandra and Kevin maritally. Kevin began to let go of the resentment he accumulated when Sandra neglected him and the kids during the early stages of Alice's disability. He also became more supportive and helpful with Alice.

Some of their marital tension was due also to Kevin's different expectations about how to care for an aging parent. Such differences between spouses are common and can present quite a stumbling block for a sandwich-generation couple.

Kevin's model was the opposite of Sandra's. His mom and dad hardly took care of their parents. He expected to offer limited financial help if necessary, but that was it. So when Sandra followed such a different model, Kevin was doubly irritated. Not only was his wife abandoning him and the kids, but for reasons that didn't make any sense to him.

When Kevin and Sandra finally listened to each other and realized that their expectations were in conflict chiefly because they were based on different family models, they were then able to hammer out a joint approach. Better to explore your expectations ahead of time, however, before problems emerge.

Then to further minimize marital resentment and conflict as your parents age, develop a game plan that reflects both your values and those of your partner. This will help keep your partner's resentment down to a minimum.

✳

**You, your spouse, and your parents will likely differ over how to care for aging parents, for duty is in the eye of the beholder. Expect those differences . . . and communicate about them.**

✳

### An Aging Parent's Frailty Can Be Difficult to Accept

Finally, your beliefs about aging and death can also enhance or compromise your ability to relate to your parents as they grow older. As your parents transition from the ranks of the "young old" to those of the "frail elderly," you lose much of the mom and dad you once knew. Their physical competence and independence begin to erode, and even basic mental abilities often falter.

This caught Edgar off guard, especially when his seventy-eight-year-old father, Antonio, began to forget bank deposits. Antonio had built a multimillion-dollar restaurant supply business from the ground up after dropping out of school in the seventh grade to help his family during the Depression. Edgar learned the business at his father's knee and had always been proud of the old man. He still expected him to visit on Christmas and to hold his own in traffic.

It was hard for him to face the fact that his father needed assistance. With three children in college and the business in full swing, Edgar didn't have time to worry about Antonio. It wasn't until Edgar's wife, Maria, confronted him with his father's failing strength that he recognized how his once powerful dad now needed his help.

Then he pitched in with determination and affection. This reassured Maria, who worried that if Edgar could be this blind and insensitive to someone he loved as much as his father, perhaps it was an omen of things to come if she ever needed his care. Her concern was valid, for the caretaking you and your spouse offer to your parents might be a precursor to how you will care for each other as you grow older.

❋

**It's difficult to accept a parent's increased frailty. How you or your partner respond may raise marital anxiety as well. "Will my partner be there for me later?" you might wonder.**

❋

## Caretaking Tips

When her eighty-five-year-old mother left the stove on overnight and nearly burned down the house, Dorothy knew it was time to intervene. She and her husband, Allen, had moved Linnea in with them after the kids left the nest, but Linnea's Alzheimer's had grown progressively worse.

They decided to put her in a home. It was a painful but necessary decision. "I liked the idea of keeping her home and caring for her," Dorothy said, "but I was so terribly exhausted. I just couldn't do it anymore."

More than one of every ten Americans over the age of sixty-five have Alzheimer's. If you have a parent over the age of eighty-five or ninety (depending upon which study you read), his or her chances of getting Alzheimer's are 50 percent. So what do you do when someone in your family has Alzheimer's or some other disabling condition that requires round-the-clock care?

The first thing when making a decision is to explore all the options, even if some look impossible.  Don't limit your choices prematurely, for you can end up feeling trapped or helpless. The more leeway you give yourself, the more empowered you'll feel when you do make a decision.

Be sure to contact local agencies for help and advice. This is their specialty, and they can give you valuable information you might not have considered. They also don't operate on myths, which tend to run in families—things like, "Remember

Uncle Jed died after his kids sent him to that nursing home."
No one mentions he was ninety-one and had dementia.

Involve your spouse when making a decision as well. This
is not the time for unilateral action. Taking care of aging parents requires time, financial support, and emotional en-
durance. Do your research, talk with your partner, and set up
a realistic plan for yourself and your family. Also, let yourself
sit with the decision for a week or two before taking action.

In addition, be realistic. If you really want your mother or father to move in with you, and you can handle it emotionally,
physically, and maritally, go for it. But if after looking at the options realistically you realize you can't do it, don't put yourself
down. That creates more internal conflict, which can worsen
your emotional or physical health. Remember, too, that what
works for some couples might not work for you. Allow yourself
to be who you are and respect your personal limits.

Dorothy had reached hers when she put her mother in that
nursing home. For Dorothy, it was when her mother nearly
burned down the house. But her mother's increasing loss of
bladder and bowel control was also a factor. For other couples,
putting a parent in a nursing home may depend on how much
the parent wanders or how combative or violent he or she becomes. When an aging parent can't recognize the family or can
no longer walk are also key turning points for many "sandwich"
couples.

Choosing a good institution is a challenge as well. Besides
looking for a clean and secure environment where patients
can't wander away or get hurt, it's also important to look for
a good activities program and a facility that has a well-trained
staff. Because more than half of all nursing home residents
have Alzheimer's disease, odds are good that the staff will have

received some specialized training in how to handle the confused elderly and how to talk to them. Still, spend a day at a nursing home and talk to residents and family members before placing a loved one there.

❈

**When your parents need intensive care, explore all options, consult with your partner, and respect your personal limitations. Take advantage of experts at local agencies too.**

❈

## *Take Care of Yourself to Prevent Burnout*

Whatever you do with Mom or Dad, take care of yourself while you do it. One of the biggest challenges when caring for an aging parent is burnout. It does no one any good, least of all your dependent and frail mother or father, if *you* fall apart. Take care of yourself so you can continue to take care of your aging parents.

Develop and commit yourself to a self-care plan that is realistic and respects your time and financial limitations. If you supervise a parent at home, try to get out of the house for at least an hour every day. You'll need that time away to replenish your emotional and physical batteries. Check with local agencies; many provide respite care.

At the top of your list, include exercise, like regular walks, for instance. It's the most effective thing you can do to change a bad mood, raise energy, and reduce tension, according to a recent study in the *Journal of Personality and Social Psychology*. Exercise gets your heart rate up, and you liberate endorphins and enkephalins, the body's internal morphine system. You can get an exercise high if you go long and hard enough.

Other top strategies, according to the study, include music, social interaction, which is especially helpful for you women, and changing your thinking, like giving yourself a pep talk or praying. Make sure you get adequate nutrition and rest as well.[3]

*

**If you care for an aging parent, take care of yourself, so you don't burn out. Develop a self-care plan that gets you out of the house for an hour a day, and include exercise.**

*

### Prevent Marital Burnout, Too

It's also important to create a marital-care plan to protect your relationship from the additional stress of caring for an aging parent. This is particularly significant for sandwich-generation wives, who usually assume most of the caretaking burden.

If you're a woman in the middle juggling a dependent parent with family and job responsibilities, support at home may be more important than you think, according to a recent study funded by the National Institute on Aging.[4] How stressed out or depressed you wives get, according to the researchers, is definitely affected by your marriage.

So husbands, take note: Your support is both needed and appreciated. Your wife will likely want you to listen as she explores the stress and complexity of what she's going through as a caretaker.

You wives, on the other hand, would be well advised to give your husband some space if he's the primary caretaker. Don't pry or demand that he share his feelings about his mom or dad, for instance. Both of you, however, should beware that *your* spouse, male or female, might not fit the stereotype. So when in doubt, check it out; ask your partner how you could best help.

Whatever your gender, mind your own business when it comes to how your partner handles his or her parents. Your spouse might act in ways you don't agree with, but if they don't directly affect you, give your mate the respect and consideration to handle things as he or she sees fit.

It's okay to be a good consultant and to give your mate your opinion, but only once. Then drop it, and don't nag or demean your spouse's decision. Resist the temptation to criticize your in-laws as well, especially now that they're older and more physically or emotionally limited.

If your spouse is the primary caretaker, lower your expectations and cut your mate some slack, especially during difficult times, such as a health crisis. Whether your partner is fully responsible for an older parent's care or only visits weekly, a simple demand can be the straw that breaks his or her back. Practice being a good friend during times of high stress and wait till things calm down before you ask for personal time and attention.

The bottom line: Keep your relationship alive by taking good care of each other. Do a chore your partner usually does or take charge of planning a night out. Don't be afraid to remind your partner to take it easy now and then, but do it gently. You're likely to see the physical and emotional warning signs of stress before your spouse does.

Besides being considerate, your marital-care plan should include spending time together in a stress-free activity of mutual interest. It's also essential that when you communicate your needs, you don't attack. If you feel neglected by your partner's busy schedule, get below your anger to your feelings of loneliness, for instance. They're much easier to hear.

❀

**Develop a marital-care plan to prevent relationship burnout.**
**Support the caretaking spouse, mind your own business,**
**lower your expectations, and take extra care of each other.**

❀

Sandwiched between exiting children and aging parents, you're likely to navigate this difficult marital transition during a time of high stress. You can't prevent the curves midlife throws at you, but with realistic expectations, good communication, and basic consideration, this difficult passage can renew and strengthen your relationship.

### CHAPTER 10

# Career Changes and Retirement

Grow old along with me! The best is yet to be.
—Robert Browning

Despite Browning's poetic optimism, the best seemed a long way off, as far as Dirk and Sally were concerned.

"You know those angry white males everybody talks about, the guys you hear on Rush Limbaugh, well sign me up!" Dirk raised his fist in the air like an angry football coach midway through a losing season.

Like most of the dual-earning couples who make up almost half the workforce, Dirk and Sally worked harder than ever before, but retirement was nowhere in sight.

"I feel like Charlie Chaplin in that movie where he can't keep up with the treadmill," he continued. "I'm moving as fast as I can, but I keep losing ground."

So are millions of other baby boomers. Four out of five individuals didn't think they would have enough money to retire, in a study of 1,800 mostly middle-aged Americans. Almost half thought they will need either full- or part-time work to support themselves during their retirement years.[1]

At fifty-one years old, Dirk was not only losing ground, he was losing his wife's support as well. "This is getting old," she complained, pointing to Dirk as he raised his voice as well as his fist. "He's been like this for the last two years, and frankly, I can't take it anymore." Sally's anger gave way to sadness as she reached in front of her husband for a Kleenex.

"Money. That's our marriage problem," she added. "It's bringing Dirk down and tearing us apart." She nervously twisted her tissue and continued. "I worry about the bills, too," she admitted. "We're drowning in a river of debt, and the water keeps rising." With too many expenses already and two kids yet to get through college, Dirk and Sally were waist deep and only midway through their marital crossing.

## Work, Money, and Marriage at Midlife

Unfortunately, Dirk and Sally's financial problems are not unusual. Like the majority of today's working couples, according to the national Study of the Changing Workforce, their household income wasn't any better than that of families twenty years earlier, when typically only husbands worked outside the home.[2] This despite the fact that both Dirk and Sally work full-time.

In addition, Dirk and Sally probably *do* work harder than ever before. Whereas only a third of workers in 1977 reported bringing work home, now half of all workers do. They also work more hours; the average work week is now more than forty-seven hours long.

Dirk and Sally were right: Much of their marital tension was due to work and financial stress, and much of that was a reflection of the changing workplace.

❋

**Dual-earning couples make up almost half the workforce.**
**Employees also work longer for less pay than they**
**did twenty years ago. This is especially challenging**
**if you're now at midlife.**

❋

### Increasing Stress at Work

Put it all together, and the increase of stress at work can affect your relationship at home. In fact, that same study found that half of today's workers experienced either some or a lot of interference between their job and family life. This was certainly true for Dirk and Sally.

Twenty years ago, however, only a third of America's workers reported similar levels of interference. This is probably due to the fact that many women now work outside the home, making it difficult for parents to balance work and child care. It's no surprise, according to another study of several hundred dual-earning couples, that today's working parents overwhelmingly want greater flexibility on the job.

Not only does the work itself cause more tension and conflict at home, but job insecurity is up as well. This, too, worried Dirk and Sally and contributed to their relationship stress.

Although Sally had a stable job with the state, Dirk managed a restaurant for an unpredictable and explosive owner.

He was paid well, but the emotional abuse and job insecurity definitely took their toll. He never knew from one month to the next whether he'd be fired or not. Dirk's anxiety, unfortunately, is also reflected in the worplace at large; twice as many workers today fear losing their jobs compared to employees twenty years ago.

Worse still, those fears often come to pass. When they do, it can be especially tough on middle-aged middle managers like Dirk when they try to get rehired. Whereas workers under thirty-five take roughly three months to get back to work, according to a recent study by the American Management Association, if you're between forty-five and fifty-four years of age, it takes an average of six months to find a new job. Not only that, but younger workers make *more* money when they return to work, while middle-aged workers make *less*.[3]

❋

**Your work is more likely to interfere with your family life today compared to twenty years ago. You're also twice as likely to be worried about losing your job now as well.**

❋

### *Your Work Needs Change at Midlife*

Money, however, isn't the whole story. Work fulfills other needs as well, and many of them change as you move through midlife.

For instance, career decisions made when you were

younger, often to please parents, may change during your middle years. This was a key factor for Sally. Her parents had never encouraged her to go to college. It was always assumed that she would get married and become a homemaker.

But once her children began school, Sally decided to go back to school herself to become a licensed dietitian. During her thirties, she had become increasingly interested in nutrition and health. She loved reading about vitamins and dietary supplements. She even taught a nutrition class in the evening at her children's preschool. For Sally, her job as a dietitian for the state department of education was a dream come true and meant a lot more to her than just a paycheck.

Dirk, too, despite his financial frustration, made a career transition during his middle years that he was still pleased with today. Soon after their second child was born, he decided to move out of Los Angeles so he could raise his children in the country. Although it had been a struggle financially, he loved fishing and hiking with his kids, and now that they were teenagers, he was also glad they were safe from much of the gang violence in L.A.

Freud said that the two tasks of adulthood were love and work. We've challenged you throughout this book not to shrink from change in your intimate relationship during your middle years. You should do no less with work. It is a huge part of who you are; much of your identity, purpose, and meaning comes from work.

If your work doesn't provide you with opportunity or a sense of accomplishment, you have choices. Change jobs, start a business, go back to school, explore a new career. True, change is always fraught with risk. But to remain stagnant, frustrated, and resentful is an invitation for depression and despair . . . at any age.

As a friend of ours told us before she lost her battle with breast cancer: Life is not a dress rehearsal; you have to live it now.

*

**Just as your needs change in your intimate relationship, so will your needs at work. It is too big a part of you to ignore. Have the courage to change jobs, or even your career, if necessary.**

*

## *Work Stress Can Trigger Marital Conflict*

Stress or depression due to work can be especially challenging for husbands, because a good deal of what defines a man is often his job. But as two-income households become the rule rather than the exception, and as women take over more of the new high-growth jobs, many traditionally male-dominated industries, such as shipbuilding, are in decline.

Put it all together, and it can challenge a man's masculinity, according to studies reviewed in a monthly publication of the American Psychological Association. In order not to feel like today's second sex, psychologists suggest two things. First, focus on what you're competent at, whether that's fixing the family cars or being a gourmet cook. Second, look at today's transition as an opportunity.[4]

The manager of the Chevron station in our town agrees,

especially about seeing working women as an opportunity. "We've worked so many years supporting them, it's about time they supported us for a while," he said with a chuckle. That can be more challenging on the male ego than it sounds, however. According to the Families and Work Institute, 55 percent of women who work in the United States provide at least half of their family's income.

Another potential battle ground is when one of you wants to change careers at midlife. Wives, don't be surprised if your husband feels threatened by your increased independence, particularly your additional contact with other men. Husbands, be sensitive to your wife's financial anxiety if you contemplate a risky career move midstream. Remember to use the communication skills you learned in part 3, especially listening.

If your spouse has a different level of ambition than you do, however, you're probably better off working on your self-talk, rather than talking to your partner. Trying to change such a core personality trait will more likely frustrate both you and your spouse rather than yield any positive results.

Change how you talk to yourself as well if you're jealous of your partner's enthusiasm for work. Just because your spouse enjoys his or her job doesn't mean your mate loves you any less. It frequently has little to do with you. Don't expect to fulfill all your partner's needs for social contact, purpose, self-worth, or intellectual stimulation.

If your spouse becomes disabled and can't work, that will likely affect your marriage too. Short periods of disability are more common during midlife than you might think. Don't be surprised if your patience gives way to resentment after some time. Your disabled partner, meanwhile, besides growing depressed, is also likely to lose patience with you.

❋

**From disability to differing levels of ambition, work
can impact your marriage in a variety of ways.
Men, especially, are identified with work and can be
particularly sensitive to failure.**

❋

### The Ten Commandments of Coping with Work Stress

Rather than let stress at work affect you or your relationship, here are what we call the Ten Commandments of Coping with Work Stress. The first five, by the way, were taught to congressional aides by psychologists at a stress management seminar hosted by the American Psychological Association.[5]

1. *Exercise.* Do it during your lunch hour or at the end of your workday. Even a twenty-minute walk can help leave stress where it belongs—at work. Exercise ensures that you arrive home relaxed, even if you do it midday. It also helps to get up and stretch periodically as well.

2. *Breathe deeply for relaxation.* Close your eyes or stare blankly ahead and take three slow, deep breaths. Feel your muscles, like tight rubber bands, loosen and let go. It takes less than a minute, literally. Try it now and see for yourself!

3. *Maintain a positive attitude.* Review chapter 4 and do the four-step at work. Identify your triggers, faulty assumptions, and consequences. Then come up with realistic reinterpreta-

tions. Remember: Change how you think, and you can change how you feel.

4. *Delay action until your emotion subsides.* Whether it's your marital mate or your office mate, counting to ten is back in vogue. "Vent the pent," especially with the boss, usually gets you in trouble. Build in a delay, so that if you decide to take action, it'll be well thought out.

5. *Find supportive colleagues.* It's one thing to delay, but another to isolate yourself emotionally. Research shows that friends can be good medicine. Talking to supportive colleagues can help you let off steam, clarify your feelings, collect your thoughts, and preserve your health.

6. *Develop empathy.* Even your boss has a legitimate point of view. Like in marriage, if you can see the other guy's perspective, you're less likely to feel unjustly attacked, victimized, or abused.

7. *Listen.* If it works miracles at home, why not try it at work? It's especially powerful when supervisors, colleagues, or clients are upset. They won't need to attack if they feel like they're being heard.

8. *Be assertive.* Obviously, you can't set too many limits with your boss, but you can set some. "Just say no" is a powerful way to avoid stress from piling up and overwhelming you, at work or at home.

9. *Sort out what you can and can't change.* Apply the Serenity Prayer from chapter 7 to stress at work: "God, grant me the serenity to accept the things I cannot change, the courage to change the things I can, and the wisdom to know the difference."

10. *Develop your personal life.* If you can't change much at work, and you can't afford to change your job or career, enrich

your life on the outside. A psychologist friend of ours who works at a mental hospital for the criminally insane surfs every chance he gets. Learn to have fun, individually and as a couple.

❋

**Try the Ten Commandments of Coping with Work Stress.**
**Exercise, breathe deeply, maintain a positive**
**attitude, and delay acting impulsively, for example.**
**Also, listen and assert yourself.**

❋

## Prevent Work and Money from Distressing Your Relationship

If you struggle with work or financial stress at midlife, it doesn't have to tear apart your marriage. It's like any other challenge to your relationship: Either change how you talk to yourself, or talk to your partner more effectively.

Those were the two tools Dirk and Sally used to repair their marital foundation. For openers, Dirk needed to become more aware of his aggressive style of communication and how it overwhelmed his wife, Sally.

He learned to keep his tirades short and his volume low so his wife didn't need to withdraw from him. He began to check his audience as well to make sure they were still interested and listening. If Sally wasn't, for instance, that was a clue that perhaps he had talked for too long.

In addition, Dirk also learned to knock on the door *before* bursting into Sally's psychological space. For instance, he now asked, "Is this a good time to talk?" rather than assuming he could barge in verbally any time he wanted. Because Sally felt respected and empowered, she was less likely to withdraw or abandon him emotionally.

Besides learning how to talk to Sally more effectively, Dirk also needed to talk to himself more competently. He tended to "awfulize" and "catastrophize" about work and money. As he learned to handle his anxiety more successfully, Sally felt less burdened, resentful, and distant.

Although he wasn't a writer by nature, he tried jotting down his thoughts and feelings before speaking them out loud. This helped him clarify issues and lessened the likelihood that he would burn out Sally as a listener. It also prevented him from inappropriately blaming her when he felt overwhelmed or threatened at work.

Sally, for her part, learned to assert her limits rather than passively hope that Dirk would read her mind and know when she needed a break. This prevented her from continuing to build up resentment toward Dirk, which would later show up as distance and disdain. Both needed to agree on a plan of action to tackle financial problems.

As they learned to communicate more effectively, Sally became more of a willing participant and partner, rather than the passive victim who would then sabotage Dirk's unilateral decisions. As their financial planning became more bilateral and their agreements more win-win, they began to cope more productively with their fiscal stress and anxiety and to dig themselves out of their financial hole.

❋

**To prevent work and money from distressing your
relationship, talk to yourself differently and
your partner more effectively. The bottom lines
are still self-talk and communication.**

❋

# Retirement

"Ever since Tom retired, I feel like I'm in jail," Doris said sadly.
Her eyes stared vacantly out the window like a prisoner might
look at distant train tracks extending over the horizon.

"It's strange really, all those years when the kids were little,
how I couldn't wait for Tom to get home from work," she reflected. "Now he's home all the time, and it's driving me
crazy!"

Doris's story is not strange, however. In fact, we see it all the
time. Many husbands, once so vital and productive, come
home and roost. Although they tinker in the yard or out in the
garage, for wives who were used to a lot of independence, it
can be smothering and confining.

For his part, Tom felt hurt, unwanted, and abandoned.
"We've been married thirty-five years, and suddenly I don't
know who Doris is anymore," he said sadly. He took an early
retirement as a marketing executive for a major appliance
manufacturer and tried to get into golf and fishing, but he was
bored and depressed. His depression, in turn, was rocking the
marital boat.

## *Depression Can Affect Husbands and Marriages at Retirement*

According to a study in the journal *Psychology and Aging,* how satisfied you are with your retirement will affect whether you get depressed or not, and *that* will affect your marital satisfaction.[6] The study highlighted three strategies that can help you retire successfully, none of which Tom had going for him. First, he didn't structure his time, so he had no sense of daily direction or accomplishment. Second, he hadn't built any new social contacts. And finally, he had no sense of purpose in his life overall.

No wonder he was depressed. He was also very lonely. He had contact at the bank, gas station, and hardware store, but nothing like he had when he was working. This, too, according to the research, played a significant role in his depression. For loneliness isn't so much related to how *much* contact you have, but the *quality* of your interactions with others.[7]

Sometimes it's you wives who get depressed after retirement, especially if you feel hemmed in by your husband. But the bottom line for you husbands is pretty clear: Don't expect your wife to fill the emotional void after you retire. If you're restless, get out of the house and get a life. Your wife probably has one already. You need to find one too . . . separate from hers.

❋

**Wives can feel crowded by husbands after retirement,
especially if the men are depressed. To combat depression,
structure your time, build new relationships,
and find a sense of purpose.**

❋

## Women and Retirement

Like many women, Doris had a life beyond her work. Besides caring for her aging mother and visiting her daughter and grandchildren, she especially enjoyed her freedom.

"I don't want to go back in the kitchen and make Tom tuna sandwiches," she said angrily. "Been there, done that," she added.

Although she retired from teaching three years before Tom ended his career, many women continue to work after their husbands retire. Because most join the workforce later than their husbands, many still advance in their careers or find work emotionally fulfilling during their fifties and sixties.

Studies show that women who work outside the home are frequently less depressed and have higher self-esteem than women who don't. Many enjoy the social camaraderie and meaning it provides, especially after the nest empties.

If you continue to work after your husband retires, this can challenge your relationship, however. Your husband may feel cheated and neglected. The good news, though, is that it gives both of you important time away from each other. Still, be prepared for some hard feelings, and remember to listen them down.

❀

**Some women work after their husbands retire because
they began their careers later or find work stimulating.
Be prepared, however, to listen down your
husband's feelings of neglect.**

❀

## Becoming Grandparents

Besides retirement, another shift in the landscape during later midlife is the addition of grandchildren. It is a time of reflection, as you pass the baton to the next generation, both at work and within your family. A major transition is occurring, as you move from the summer of productivity to the poignancy of your autumn years.

You are not yet old, but you also sense that it is not too far away. You rock the children of your children in perhaps the same chair you were rocked in by your own parents. You're not quite ready for the rocker yourself, but you grow more philosophical in your approach to life. As the poet William Blake wrote, "The child's toys and the old man's reasons are the fruits of the two seasons."

Becoming a grandparent can also bring you closer to your adult child and his or her partner. But beware of becoming too intrusive. This is especially true for you moms. Although *you* may view your grandchildren as part of your extended family, according to a recent study, your children may not. They often view their own spouses and children as a separate family unit.[8]

Be sensitive to this difference, call before visiting, and ask your adult children periodically if they would like more space.

There can be other problems as well. If you're a stepparent, for instance, your spouse will likely be more generous and involved with his or her grandchildren than you will. This can trigger feelings of jealousy or conflict over finances. Try to see it from your partner's point of view and remember to get below your anger and to listen to your spouse's perspective.

An even bigger challenge is the increasing possibility that you may actually *raise* your grandchildren for a period of time. More than three million children live with grandparents or other relatives, according to the American Association of Retired Persons, due to teen pregnancy, substance abuse, child abuse or neglect, and other factors. That's up 40 percent over the last decade. If it happens to you, seek professional support.

❉

**Grandchildren may arrive at about the same time you retire. It is a poignant time of reflection as you pass the baton to the next generation both at work and in your family.**

❉

### Preparing Emotionally for Retirement

You often hear how important it is to prepare financially for retirement. But are you prepared emotionally as well? And what if you and your partner disagree?

For instance, your partner might want to compromise financially and retire earlier than you would like, especially if your spouse is dissatisfied with his or her career or current job. Or your mate might desire more time together as a couple than you would prefer.

If you're a dual-career couple, and especially if you continue to work after your husband retires, don't be surprised if you switch provider and homemaker roles. Who's in charge is often determined by who's bringing home the bacon.

Retirement also challenges how you define yourself. This was at the root of Tom's depression, if you remember. You may lose considerable social power and prestige once you're no longer a doctor, lawyer, or Indian chief. Tom had prepared financially for retirement, but he hadn't planned ahead emotionally.

It's also important to communicate as a couple. Retirement is an excellent time to get away for a weekend and have a State of the Union. The bottom line is that the more things change, the more you have to talk about. Better to communicate ahead of time than after the fact.

❋

**You may be prepared financially for retirement, but are you prepared emotionally as well? Communication is crucial: The greater the change, the more things you need to talk over.**

❋

### The Seven Steps to Successful Retirement

Communication is important, but there are other things you need to do in order to retire succesfully. Let's begin, however, with revisiting the importance of talking things over with your partner.

1. *Communicate*. At each major step of midlife change, the mobile shifts dramatically. You and your partner have much to renegotiate, and plenty to disagree about. Better to do so *before* retirement, as well as after.

2. *Plan ahead*. If you can, retire in stages. Nearly three-fourths of workers surveyed during their fifties said they would prefer to retire gradually, rather than all at once like their parents did.[9] Work part-time, for instance; it'll help get your feet wet.

3. *Be realistic*. Talk to yourself realistically about your retirement expectations. This includes being flexible when things don't go as planned. They won't, you know.

4. *Structure your time*. You want freedom, but you also need structure. Provide yourself with daily direction and challenge yourself to get things done. Even small accomplishments are important.

5. *Follow your passion*. You'll need a new dream, a reason for being, something to wrap your life around. As Nietzsche said, "He who has a *why* to live can bear almost any *how*."

6. *Have the courage to change*. It took courage to ride your first bike, even though you knew you'd take a few spills. You rode anyway. Art Linkletter was right when he said, "Old age is not for sissies."

7. *Get involved*. Cultivate new interests; join a bike club, or go to church or temple, for instance. Have lunch with friends. Studies show that if you connect with others, you'll be less depressed, and even live longer.

✱

**Take the Seven Steps to Successful Retirement. Communicate,
plan ahead, but be realistic and structure your time.
Also follow your passion, have the courage
to change, and get involved.**

✱

## Successful Aging

"Find something that you enjoy and you believe in," fitness guru Jack LaLanne told us during a TV interview. "This is what keeps you alive." It was difficult to argue with an eighty-year-old man who did push-ups on his fingers for the camera. "You have seventy trillion cells in your body," he continued, "and every one of those cells is stimulated by your brain."

The research agrees, strongly and consistently, with La-Lanne's bottom line: "Move it or lose it." This applies to your brain as well as your body.

One study, for instance, split up 175 older people into two groups. One was the control group, whose lives stayed pretty much the same. The other group became foster grandparents and had to walk several miles a day. The foster grandparents had more complex brain activity, slept better, and had better memories compared to the control subjects, who hadn't been challenged.[10]

When the American Psychological Association reviewed several studies on aging, they found that some forms of memory actually improve with age. But here, too, "move it or lose it" is the key. The more complex and stimulating your life is, the more likely you are to be mentally alert, including having a better memory.[11]

Take those retired folks who travel around in RVs. When researchers compared couples who frequently traveled in RVs with those who didn't, they found that the RV couples were happier, healthier, and more mentally alert.[12]

But you don't have to ramble around the continent to stay sharp mentally. Just mow the lawn or go back to school, according to psychologists at several universities, including Harvard and Yale, who followed 1,200 older people for more than two and a half years. Education and exercise, according to their study, are the best ways to prevent cognitive decline.[13]

So as you near the end of your middle years, remember to challenge yourself—physically and mentally. The rest of your life depends on it.

❋

**If you want to age successfully, stretch your mind as well as your body. "Move it or lose it," according to the research, keeps you physically in shape and mentally sharp.**

❋

Tom and Doris, by the way, eventually worked out their differences. Therapy provided them with an opportunity to review their State of the Union. Tom was able to hear that Doris's need for space and independence wasn't because she didn't love him.

As he "got a life," their marital mobile righted itself again. Tom had always enjoyed singing, but he never had the time to pursue it during his younger adulthood. Once he joined a choir, bought an organ, and began to perform at convalescent centers, however, he was a changed man. As Doris wryly put it, "He's busy like he's in his right mind."

The key for Tom, as is often the case for men at retirement, was to find a new path with heart and to get involved. Not a bad lesson to learn at any age.

In closing, we'd like to thank you for inviting us into your home. We hope that you picked up a skill or two to help you renew your marriage at midlife. It's not easy to continue to rekindle an ongoing intimate relationship. In fact, it's probably one of the most difficult of life's endeavors.

It takes courage to risk being who you are, especially when how you've changed or who you've become may threaten your partner. Do it anyway, and do it repeatedly. But remember to listen with sensitivity to your spouse's concerns too.

Remember, also, to take advantage of the counseling professional. You might need a midwife to help you in the rebirth of your relationship. The sooner you come in, the more likely we'll be able to help.

Best of luck.

# Notes

## CHAPTER 1

1. Laura Carstensen, John Gottman, and Robert Levenson, "Emotional Behavior in Long-Term Marriage," *Psychology and Aging* 10, no. 1 (1995), pp. 140–49.

2. Eva Klohnen, Elizabeth Vandewater, and Amy Young, "Negotiating the Middle Years: Ego Resiliency and Successful Midlife Adjustment in Women," *Psychology and Aging* 11, no. 3 (1996), pp. 431–42.


## CHAPTER 2

1. Scott Silberman and Sharon Robinson-Kurpius, "Relationships Among Love, Marital Satisfaction and Duration of Marriage," paper presented at the annual convention of the American Psychological Association, 1997.

2. Annette Mahoney and Ken Pargament, "Sacred Vows:

The Sanctification of Marriage and Its Psychosocial Implications," paper presented at the annual convention of the American Psychological Association, 1997.

### CHAPTER 3

1. Fritz Perls, *Gestalt Therapy Verbatim* (Lafayette, CA: Real People Press, 1969).

2. Teresa Davis, "Gender Differences in Masking Negative Emotions: Ability or Motivation?" *Developmental Psychology* 31, no. 4 (1995), pp. 660–67.

3. Reuven Bar-On and Steven Stein, "Men and Women Have Different Kinds and Levels of Emotional Intelligence," Multi-Health Systems, 1997.

4. Erik Erikson, *Childhood and Society* (New York: W. W. Norton, 1950).

5. Anthony de Mello, *The Way to Love* (New York: Image Books/Doubleday, 1992).

### CHAPTER 4

1. Victoria Medvec, Scott Madey, and Thomas Gilovich, "When Less Is More: Counterfactual Thinking and Satisfaction Among Olympic Medalists," *Journal of Personality and Social Psychology* 69, no. 4 (1995), pp. 603–10.

2. Gary Snyder, *The Practice of the Wild* (San Francisco: North Point, 1990).

### CHAPTER 6

1. Carl Rogers, *On Becoming a Person* (Boston: Houghton Mifflin, 1961).

2. Robert Alberti and Michael Emmons, *Your Perfect Right* (San Luis Obispo, CA: Impact, 1970).

3. Thomas Gordon, *Parent Effectiveness Training* (New York: Peter Wyden, 1970).

#### CHAPTER 8

1. Ellen Frank and Carol Anderson, Family Therapy Institute of the Western Psychiatric Institute and Clinic, 1979.

#### CHAPTER 9

1. G. Spitze and J. Logan, "More Evidence on Women (and Men) in the Middle," *Research on Aging* 12 (1990), pp. 182–98.

2. Victor Cicirelli, "Attachment and Obligation as Daughters' Motives for Caregiving Behavior and Subsequent Effect on Subjective Burden," *Psychology and Aging* 8, no. 2 (1993), pp. 144–55.

3. Robert Thayer, J. Robert Newman, and Tracey McClain, "Self-Regulation of Mood: Strategies for Changing a Bad Mood, Raising Energy, and Reducing Tension," *Journal of Personality and Social Psychology* 67, no. 5 (1994), pp. 910–25.

4. Mary Ann Parris Stephens and Aloen Townsend, "Stress of Parent Care: Positive and Negative Effects on Women's Other Roles," *Psychology and Aging* 12, no. 2 (1997), pp. 376–86.

#### CHAPTER 10

1. Study by Sun America, Inc., reported by CNN, April 1, 1998.

2. Study presented by Ellen Galinski, president of Families and Work Institute, February 1998.

3. Kathy Bergen, "Mid-management Now in Bloom," *Chicago Tribune*, March 1998.

4. Nathan Seppa, "What Defines a Man Today?" *APA Monitor*, 1997.

5. Frank Cavaliere, "Capitol Hill Staff Gets Tips on Reducing Stress," *APA Monitor*, 1995.

6. Susan Higginbottom, Julian Barling, and E. Kevin Kelloway, "Linking Retirement Experiences and Marital Satisfaction: A Meditational Model," *Psychology and Aging* 8, no. 4 (1993), pp. 508–16.

7. John Nezlek, Mark Imbrie, and Glenn Shean, "Depression and Everyday Social Interaction," *Journal of Personality and Social Psychology* 67, no. 6 (1994), pp. 1101–11.

8. Karen Fingerman, "Sources of Tension in the Aging Mother and Adult Daughter Relationship," *Psychology and Aging* 11, no. 4 (1996), pp. 591–606.

9. "Health and Retirement Study" funded by the National Institute on Aging and reported in "Retirement Can Open Up a Wealth of Opportunities," *APA Monitor*, 1996.

10. Pamela Margoshes, "For Many, Old Age Is the Prime of Life," *APA Monitor*, 1995.

11. Beth Azar, "Some Forms of Memory Improve as People Age," *APA Monitor*, 1996.

12. David and Dorothy Counts, research presented at the American Anthropological Association, 1996.

13. Marilyn Albert, Cary Savage, Kenneth Jones, Lisa Berkman, Teresa Seeman, Dan Blazer, and John Rowe, "Predictors of Cognitive Change in Older Persons: MacArthur Studies of Successful Aging," *Psychology and Aging* 10, no. 4 (1995), pp. 568–89.

# Index

10 circ
1-6-06

| | | DATE DUE | SSCCA | 306 |
|---|---|---|---|---|
| | | | | .81 |
| | | | | B864 |
| | | | | |
| BRODY, STEVE | | | | |
| RENEWING YOUR | | | | |
| MARRIAGE AT MIDLIFE | | | | |
| | | | | |
| | | 1999 | | 1/8 |
| | | | | |
| | | | | |

SSCCA     306
          .81
          B864


HOUSTON PUBLIC LIBRARY
CENTRAL LIBRARY
                        11/12

          3-4-99